OPTIMIZE ME

The Guide to Better Health, Wealth & Happiness

JACK ANSTANDIG, MD & RANDY CARVER CRPC®

outskirtspress
DENVER, COLORADO

Outskirts Press, Inc.
http://www.outskirtspress.com

Paperback ISBN: 978-1-4787-2356-1

Outskirts Press and the "OP" logo are trademarks belonging to Outskirts Press, Inc.

PRINTED IN THE UNITED STATES OF AMERICA

"The authors dedicate this book to you, the reader, and the seeker of health, wealth and happiness. We wish you all the best in all things and appreciate the opportunity to be your partner and privileged to be part of your journey!"

Randy Carver, CRPC®
Jack Anstandig, MD

IMPORTANT NOTICE

This information contained in this book is intended to serve as a basis for further discussion with your professional advisors. Great effort has been taken to provide accurate information which has been obtained from sources believed to be accurate; however, there is no guarantee that the foregoing material is accurate or complete. This book should not be relied upon for preparing tax returns, starting an exercise or diet program, estate planning, or making investment decisions. Each person's needs and objectives are unique and therefore you should always consult with your medical, tax, legal, or financial advisor before making any medical, tax, legal or investment decisions

Any opinions are those of Randy Carver and Jack Anstandig and not RJFS or Raymond James Financial Services Inc. Expressions of opinion are as of 12/20/13 and are subject to change without notice. This information is not intended as a solicitation. Past performance may not be indicative of future results.

Contents

Introduction 1

Chapter 1: What Is Your Vision? 5

Chapter 2: Where Are We?. 22

Chapter 3: Where Are You Going? 26

Chapter 4: What Got You Here Won't Get You There 31

Chapter 5: The Action Plan 38

Chapter 6: Modes of Change - Vehicles 44

Chapter 7: Protecting Your Greatest Asset 51

Chapter 8: How Much Do I Need? Key Benchmarks 56

Chapter 9: The Decisions We Make 60

Chapter 10: Road Hazards.. 64

Chapter 11: Selecting Advisors 72

Chapter 12: Your Health 80

Chapter 13: Your Wealth 84

Chapter 14: Happiness 86

Chapter 15: Master Trip Planner 91

Chapter 16: Starting Thoughts 98

About the Authors 102

Appendix I: Key Estate Planning Documents & Checklist 105

Appendix 2: Will You Outlive Your Money? 120

Appendix 3: Budget & Income 125

Appendix 4: Emergency Savings – Reserve 131

Appendix 5: Long Term Care Insurance 133

Appendix 6: Diet and Exercise 139

Index 143

Introduction

You can be happier, healthier and more financially secure regardless of where you are today. The good news is that what we do will impact our future more than our circumstances. The question is whether you live life by default or by design? How can you ensure that you can live the life you desire? Have you ever wondered why some people are phenomenally successful when others with better technical skills, opportunities and funding are not? Why are some people so successful despite seeming insurmountable challenges and others who have every advantage are much less so? Success leaves clues and the results may be duplicated if someone has the desire, knowledge and discipline to do so. You clearly have the desire as you have taken the first step of reading this book. The book will provide the knowledge you need to plan and achieve your personal vision. You will learn specifically what you can do, how to do it and perhaps most importantly explore why it is important to you as you develop your personal vision plan to improve your health, wealth and happiness. You will provide the discipline for this wonderful personal journey and live life by design not by default.

Health and financial security are two important cornerstones to one's quality of life. Yes, there is no argument that love, sense of belonging, compassion, caring and happiness is the core of what we strive for to make the most out of our lives. However, with having great health and financial stability one can have the peace of mind and time to participate in the opportunities for self-fulfillment and helping others.

In this day of news overload, expert opinions are spouted out as the best thing or the new normal on any topic you can imagine. We are faced with the ever changing load of increased stress and work time consumption. Take a moment to stop and see where you stand at this very moment. With the work that you have endured for years, what do you really have to show at this point in your life? Did you ever imagine how you physically feel and look at this point in your life? If you have solid financial security, wonderful health and personal contentment you may not need to read on. Pass this book to a friend or a family member who may benefit. If you want to improve your life then read on.

It is possible and never too late to set yourself on a path of wellness and wealth relative to your realistic expectations. Navigating this route on your own can be very difficult and faced with many obstructions and dead ends. Empowering yourself with knowledge and a process, blueprint, or map can save many failed attempts, avoid frustration and help you achieve your personal vision much faster than trial and error or simply going through life without a plan. In the past information regarding health and finance was limited to professionals in the industry and not available to the average person. Today we have access to more information than ever before – it's like trying to drink out of a fire hose. Some is accurate and some is not; some relevant to your situation and some not. The usual scenario is that people get so frustrated with the excess information and where to go and want to do that nothing gets done and life just proceeds aimlessly as one continues to experience the slow erosion of their health and financial stability.

It is our hope that through the years of experience in our respective fields of health and finance, with working with thousands of people, patients and clients, we can provide a simple, logical, and successful path for you to be in the best health and have sound financial security. This will help you to best utilize all of the resources available to you for personal fulfillment and leading the life that you really want.

This book is not intended to replace working with your healthcare provider or financial professional. The purpose is to help you in developing a plan based upon your personal goals, objectives, needs and vision. This is what we do on a daily basis. Customize a plan that is specific to you and help you achieve all of your goals.

Each chapter in the book focuses on a different aspect of your journey. At the back there are appendices with detailed information on specific financial and medical topics. There is a Master Trip Planner which you can complete once the various worksheets provided throughout the book are done. This will assist you in planning your own trip and/or working with your professional healthcare and financial advisors.

"People told us they spend three to six months, and in some cases up to a year, planning a one-week vacation but not nearly as much time planning for a retirement that could last hopefully for decades." (Chris Winans, senior vice president, External Affairs at AXA Equitable press release 4/5/11). How much time do you actually spend on thinking and consistently participating in optimizing your health? Do you spend more time complaining about how you feel and worrying about your financial circumstances both now and in the near future? Congratulations on taking your first steps to make a difference for you by reading on and joining the journey to improve your life.

Why are some people so successful despite seeming insurmountable challenges and others who have every advantage are much less so? The quick answer is that they have a vision of where they want to go, an idea of where they are and a plan to make the journey. Those who are successful in all aspects of life leave clues as to how they achieve their goals. This book will give you the tools to achieve your personal health, wealth and spiritual goals whatever they may be. Ultimately, however, it is up to you whether you are successful or not.

By reading this book you have taken the first steps on your journey. Well done! We hope that you enjoy your journey and look forward to hearing from you. Your comments, questions, success stories and feedback are all welcome. You will find contact information, and some more background, for us at the back of the book.

Jack Anstandig, MD   Randy Carver, CRPC

Chapter 1: What Is Your Vision?

"A vision without a plan is just a dream. A plan without a vision is just drudgery. But a vision with a plan can change the world."
— Old Proverb

Before developing a plan to achieve your vision in general and specifically in health, wealth and personal goals you need to figure out what these goals are to give you the most out of life. If you don't know where you are going any road will lead you there. Most people don't really know what their longer term goals are and have never taken the time to think about their personal vision. You should be congratulated on taking the first step by reading this book and doing the following exercise. This is the most important thing you can do to achieve your personal goals and dreams. This process will help you define your vision for your future personally and professionally and, ultimately positively impact all aspects of your life.

As with most things that are important this process will take time and a commitment to answer the questions completely honestly and openly. The process is simple but not easy. If it were easy everyone would do it. Once you complete this process you will be ready to decide what is the best path for achieving all of your goals and dreams. You will find that your enthusiasm and drive will increase dramatically because you'll now have a clear picture of your future and a plan for taking the steps necessary for achieving your vision. In the end, you will make better more effective life decisions with a road map and an infrastructure as your foundation.

We have divided this chapter into several sections. General Life Goals, Personal Goals, Monetary, Professional, Health and Quality of Life Goals. We recommend completing this and then coming back to look at your answers after a couple of days. Make any changes you feel necessary and then leave it for a few days again. If the answers still feel right and reflect your true vision then you can move on. You don't want to spend too much time before you take action, but you need to devote the time and consideration that planning your future needs and deserves. You can write in the book or on separate paper or devices – the most important thing is to write down the answers.

"Your vision will become clear only when you look into your heart. Who looks outside, dreams.Who looks inside awakens."– Carl Jung

You have the ability to experience personal happiness and success both professionally and personally regardless of how you define success. The first key to this is knowing exactly what you want and the second is having the drive to make your vision happen. Once you have defined your goals you will have a strong enthusiasm in your personal and professional life and be on your way to living your dreams. Success will lead to more drive, energy and success. You have done the hardest part which is committing to being happy and taking steps to achieve your vision.

Once you see where you want to go you can see what specific actions are needed to get you there. More importantly you can see if how you act today is helping you move towards those goals or not. Often people are not happy in life because their behavior and actions are not consistent with their true values and desires. At the least this leads to being less productive and less happy and may lead to both physical and mental health issues.

The Big Picture

We all have our own values and beliefs that have developed over time. These dictate what is truly important to us personally, professionally and medically. By identifying what is most important to us we can define our best behavior to achieve those things. Once we identify what is important, making decisions about our behavior becomes much easier.

List the 5 things you value the most. Then list how much time per month you spend on each of these things, as a percent of your overall time.

What you value most	Time Spent	Percentage of Overall Time
1.		
2.		
3.		
4.		
5.		

List 3 things that make you unique. This may be any traits, skills or other characteristics:

1. _____

2. _____

3. _____

List 3 or more activities that you enjoy and are passionate about. List how much time you are spending on these:

1. _____

2. _____

3. _____

List 3 social issues that you are passionate about:

1. _____

2. _____

3. _____

If you could instantly achieve your dream life - what would it be? Personally, professionally and spiritually. Assume that there are no constraints - money is not an issue.

_____

_____

_____

_____

How does your life today compare to this life?

_____

_____

_____

_____

Describe how you are growing and being content spiritually. Remember there are no wrong answers!

_____

_____

_____

_____

List 3 people who are important to you and why:

1. _____

2. _____

3. _____

Look at the above and consider how much of your time you are spending on the things that are most important to you. Write your comments and thoughts here:

_____

_____

_____

_____

We will get into more detail later but write down 4 things you can do today to achieve your dream life in the future. These should be specific actions with a specific timeframe.

This is your call to action.

1. _____

2. _____

3. _____

4. _____

Have you woken up ready to tackle the day full of energy and enthusiasm and by the end of the day felt drained and unfulfilled? We can repeat that process for years and then look back and wonder what we really did to make our mark on the world. Most of us need to support ourselves financially, but are you making a difference that fulfills YOU?

_____

_____

_____

_____

Work and Career Vision

If I could do anything as a career I would....

_____

_____

_____

_____

What makes me feel fulfilled professionally is....

_____

_____

_____

I enjoy working..... (Inside, outside, city, forest, individually, part of a team, as the leader, a doer, a concept person, etc.)

_____

_____

_____

_____

How do these compare to where you are today?

_____

_____

_____

_____

What actions can you take to achieve your ideal? Be specific and list specific time frames.

_____

_____

_____

_____

Health & Medical Vision

We live in a world where beautiful people are celebrities. Their images are digitally enhanced in the media. So many people try to live to that standard. They sure look good but it is not reality! Can we really identify good health today? It is very difficult because it is so personalized due to your genetic makeup and life style, but it's what's on the inside that matters the most. Calculate the dollars in our economy that are spent on beauty and cosmetics, fashion and flair. Do you think it is significantly more or less than the money we spend on preventive health?

Look at your own spending profile. Are you committed to preventive care and a wellness plan or is health care something you only think about when you are sick? Termed more appropriately, are you reactive to sickness or proactive to wellness/health?

Take a moment and jot down a few numbers for your monthly investments.

Hair	
Beauty and Grooming Products	
Nails	
Clothes	

No one likes to be sick and we all want to live as long as we can. There is a lot more to health and wellness than avoiding illness or delaying the inevitability of death. Being healthy is core to be happy and productive. It is essential to the foundation of a successful life. None of your financial goals and personal life expectations will be achieved if you are chronically ill. You will not be operating at 100% if you are not maintaining and tuning your body, mind and spirit.

I bet you can tell when you had your oil changed faster than you can tell me when you had your teeth cleaned or your blood pressure checked. You may be very conscientious about your kid's health but what about you? Where are you on the priority list?

Here is a sobering thought: we each get one body: only one. Yes, people are getting body part improvements and replacement parts fairly often these days, but these don't "take" on a sick, unhealthy frame. If you knew you only had one pair of shoes to last you the rest of your life how well would you take care of them? If the car you are driving had to last until you were buried, would you do anything differently than you are doing today to take care of it? Do I have your attention yet??

The pace of life today makes it a challenge to maintain a healthy life style. Where do you get the time to shop for and prepare healthy meals or exercise? Maybe some things need to be changed to make room for actions that have such important long term benefits. In fact, you have the potential to accomplish great things when you are in a fit, healthy state. It radiates happiness, energy and power! "Something happen when everything is in synergy."

So, take a minute and do a personal profile on your health. Be brutally honest with yourself. This is not the time to fudge on the numbers. It's your life, after all!!

Do I feel good? ( ) Yes ( ) No Describe what you are feeling:

_____

_____

_____

_____

What are the top 3 things that impact your overall health today?

1. _____

2. _____

3. _____

What is the current state and what would you do to manage them?

Health Impacts	Current State	What are you doing?	What should you be doing?

Do you have a primary care doctor?

_____

How often do you see your doctor?

_____

_____

_____

_____

What routine maintenance do you do for your body and mind?

_____

_____

_____

_____

What 3 things would you change about your body?

1. _____

2. _____

3. _____

Would they improve your long term health?

_____

_____

_____

_____

What is your ideal picture of your health status?

_____

_____

Today

_____

_____

In 2 Years

_____

_____

In 5 Years

_____

_____

In 10 years

_____

_____

How will you achieve those goals?

_____

_____

_____

Now let's take a minute and turn to your fiscal fitness and financial status.

Financial Goals

The three most important financial goals for me are?

1. _____

2. _____

3. _____

To feel financially independent I need $_____ income per month based on the following 5 priorities:

Priority 1 Most Important	
Priority 2	
Priority 3	
Priority 4	
Priority 5	

I would like to "retire" in _____ years.

Health and Medical Goals

Weight

_____

Stamina

_____

Flexibility

_____

Energy

_____

Mind

_____

Body Composition & Structure

_____

Vitals: blood pressure, pulse, cholesterol, triglycerides, hormonal balance, nutritional status etc.

_____

Completing the Vision

I feel fulfilled and happy after I have:

_____

_____

_____

_____

If money were not an issue I would spend my time...

_____

_____

_____

_____

If I wasn't afraid I would.....

_____

_____

_____

_____

Chapter 2: Where Are We?

Before selecting the best route to achieve our personal goals and objectives we need to figure out where we are. You now have an idea of where you want to go and we will be discussing ways to get there in the next chapter. In terms of both your health and your wealth there are objective numbers to look at but also more subjective considerations. For example, you can determine your blood pressure, weight, cholesterol level, annual income and amount of savings you have, but what do these numbers mean? How do they compare to what your goal is? How do they compare to what is a reasonable or exceptional level? Is the timeframe for the goal realistic based upon where you are at? What type of route is required, versus desired, given the stated goal and your current status. First and foremost you must be honest with yourself about where you really are NOW.

Determining specific numbers is important but one does not want to become overwhelmed or suffer 'paralysis by analysis.' A good plan today is better than a perfect plan that you never implement. It is critical to be honest with yourself – saying you have more savings or income than you really have will hinder your ability to do effective planning and make real changes. The same thing is true with your medical numbers – telling yourself you weigh more or less than you do or not acknowledging a true cholesterol figure only hurts you.

How much does it cost you to maintain your standard of living today? What types of expenses do you have? Do you have any big expenses coming up? What debt do you have? What income do you have? How much can you save and invest? What is your income tax situation? Clearly there are a lot of questions and this chapter will start working through the process of figuring out where you are today. This information and the worksheets in the following pages may also be used as a tool for discussion with your healthcare and financial professionals.

With regard to your financial situation you need to look at your current assets (savings and investments), liabilities (debt such as a mortgage), income and asset protection tools (insurance, estate planning, asset titling). You will also consider future income and assets such as pensions, inheritance or deferred compensation. You should look at anticipated needs and wants for the next few years and consider how these may impact you. Finally, you need a good assessment of your income tax situation.

The first document to review is your income tax return. This will give you several critical pieces of information. First how much income you are making and second how much you are paying in taxes. Please note that if you also have income that is not reflected on the 1040 then you will want to include this as well on the worksheet provided in Appendix 3.

After filling in the expense section of the work sheet in the appendix you can do a rough check & balance as follows. First, look at your tax return and what your after tax income was – this is the amount left after you paid taxes. Now think about all of your savings (into retirement plans, the bank, etc.) and subtract this from your after tax income. The amount you are left with should be roughly equal to what you listed as your total cost of living. If there is a big difference you will want to review the figures on the expense sheet.

Your estate planning is meant to help you protect our assets and then pass them on to our heirs. Estate planning is not just about what happens after you die, but about how to protect and manage your assets while you are alive- even if you are unable or unwilling to do so. As with all of your health and financial planning, keep in mind that each person's situation is unique. We have listed the key documents everyone should consider in the appendix. We strongly recommend working with an attorney who specializes in estate planning and have included a check list and information to discuss with your estate and financial planning professional.

Determining your level of health is a more subjective exercise but is based upon objective numbers. Your healthcare provider can assist you in determining your current levels. We have included a basic sheet outlining the key metrics you should be monitoring.

Metric	Ideal	Your Score
Blood Pressure	Less than 120/80	
Cholesterol	Less than 200 mg/dL	
Fasting Blood Sugar Level	99 or less	
Body Mass Index (Measure of body weight based on weight and height)	Normal: 19-25 Overweight :26-30 Obese: Over 30	
Physical Exam	Annual	
Mammogram for	Women over 40, annual	
Prostate screening	Men over 50, annual	
Colonoscopy	Men and women over 50, earlier if there is family history	

In this chapter we have once again discussed utilizing healthcare, legal and financial professionals to assist you with your journey. The final chapter of the book will discuss considerations in hiring a professional. You may choose to utilize their services to a greater or lesser extent; however, it is up to you and only you to take control of your life and figure out where you stand today.

Chapter 3: Where Are You Going?

It has been said that a goal without a plan is just a wish. Before embarking on any journey, you need to know where you want to go. You also need to know where you are starting from and to have realistic expectations as to time and results. This is especially true for both your wealth and health planning. Often people have no specific goals and are not sure of what they are trying to do. The more specific you are with your goals the easier it is to develop your plan. For example saying you'd like to travel to Europe at some time is not a specific goal, but more of wish. Saying you would like to travel to Paris on April 24th 2018 is much easier to plan for. Saying that you want to lose weight is not a goal – saying you want to lose 25 lbs. over the next six months is a more specific goal. If you can be specific in defining a realistic endpoint then your trained experts or partner can help get you there.

As you define a specific goal you can then formulate your objectives along the path to get you there. If traveling across the country do you want a more scenic route or a more efficient one? The choice will dictate both the vehicle and the route and give you a realistic time-frame for reaching your destination. The same is true of both financial and health planning. The key is to define specific measurable goals. Saying you want to lose weight is not a goal or a plan. Saying that you will get to 125 lbs. by next July is a specific and measurable goal.

One thing that successful people do which is key to achievement of goals is framing your vision with positive, rather than negative objectives. Saying I want to weigh 125lbs is better than saying I want to lose 25 lbs. Targeting a clothing size would also be a reasonable specific goal. Other measurable objectives could also fall into place such as improving your lipid profile, lowering your blood pressure or optimizing your blood sugar control. It is not just about getting there but also maintaining or holding onto that achieved goal over time. Who wants to boomerang from 150lbs to 125lbs then back up to 160 lbs? As you will see, it is not how fast you get there, but how long can you sustain that goal.

With your retirement planning, for example, you need to decide when you want to retire and how you want to get there. It's also important to understand that retirement and specific goals are not the end of the trip, but just the beginning of a new journey. Just like a woman going through menopause , it is not the end of going through "the change", but the beginning of new health challenges with respect to mind, heart, body composition and all those factors that contribute to her overall quality of life.

Once you know where you want to go then you can begin to select the best route and vehicle. This can be great fun as everything is possible during the planning phase. With financial planning many people just pick investments without knowing where they want to go or even if the vehicle is appropriate for their individual needs and objectives. They focus on the investments rather than their vision. By focusing on your vision you can then select the most appropriate investments for YOUR needs, objectives and risk tolerance.

The same can be said for much of traditional health care today.

People are focused on symptoms and instant treatments rather than the underlying causes and long term goals. A band aid to provide a short term relief will not provide you with the resolution of the problem. For instance, lack of sleep is a major problem that many suffer from in this modern world. Yes, you can get a prescription to knock you out, but only the symptom of insomnia was temporarily solved. Why can't you sleep? What factors must be addressed to resolve this problem? How many other issues are tied into the sleeplessness? Solve the underlying problem and other mitigating factors will resolve. Sounds so simple to resolve but so few people actually attempt to fix the core issue and get distracted by the peripheral issues.

In planning we encourage you to focus on what you want to accomplish and then develop a plan; rather than having a preconceived notion of this is what you have to do because this is how things are done. Do not accept the fixed rigid framework either financially or health wise, you are unique to your own circumstances!

So where do you want to go? You have already completed some of this in the previous chapters and we have other tools to help frame your vision including an action plan in Chapter 5.

From a financial standpoint the major planning goals can be divided into short term and long term. Generally these will focus on maintaining and enhancing your standard of living in the future while being able to afford ongoing expenses. The major things people save for are retirement, children's educations and possibly health care expenses. Near term goals may be a vacation, home or vehicle purchase or family event such as a wedding.

From a health standpoint, major goals can also be divided into the major foundational goals and the minor issues which may or may not arise from dysfunctional standpoint of a weakened or impaired foundation. Common presentations which tend to be longstanding unresolved issues include fatigue, impaired sleep, anxiety, depression, poor memory, pain of some sort, reduced physical stamina, weight gain, hair loss, stomach or bowel problems or loss of sex drive to name a few. Keep in mind these are symptoms arising from a much deeper foundational issue. Examples of foundation pillars of health include nutrition, hormones, immune status, mental and cognitive function, exercise input and spiritual security.

So now take a few minutes to start outlining what your financial and health goals are. We recommend finding a quiet place and simply writing down any and everything you wish to accomplish.

Once you have all of your goals listed you will then want to divide these as near term and long term and prioritize each list. One key to achieving your goals is to have manageable objectives so you do not become overwhelmed. Keep in mind this is the start of framing your life's path in moving forward. Beginning to illustrate your health and personal financial goals will serve you well. Think about all those that just seem to be floundering and complaining about their situation. You will be on your way with a well thought out plan.

Chapter 4:
What Got You Here Won't Get You There

Driving down the road looking in the rear view mirror works until the road turns. With regard to retirement and health planning the road has already started a dramatic turn and many of the old assumptions and rules of thumb need to be re-evaluated and updated.

In this case the first curve in the road is comprised of what has been termed the Age Wave or the coming baby boomers. These are the 76 million people born between 1946 and 1964. In 2005 the first boomers were 59 ½ the age at which they could start taking penalty free withdrawals from IRA's. In 2008 the first boomers were 62 and eligible for social security benefits. There are several reasons that this necessitates a change in thinking and planning. These include but are not limited to the greater demands for retirement services by this group.

The second curve we are facing is that people are living much longer than before. When the Social Security System was signed into law by President Franklin Roosevelt in 1935, life expectancy was @ 60 years. This was a vast improvement from the turn of the century when life expectancy was age 47. None the less only 54% of the population lived to age 65.

When Medicare was added in 1965 by the Social Security Act of 1965, as part of President Lyndon B. Johnson's "Great Society" program life expectancy was just over 60 for men and 71 for women.

See chart below. Ultimately most people worked until age 65 or until they died and spent little time in retirement as we know it today.

Table 1: Life Expectancy for Social Security				
Year Cohort Turned 65	Percentage of Population Surviving from Age 21 to Age 65		Average Remaining Life Expectancy for Those Surviving to Age 65	
	Male	Female	Male	Female
1940	53.9	60.6	12.7	14.7
1950	56.2	65.5	13.1	16.2
1960	60.1	71.3	13.2	17.4
1970	63.7	76.9	13.8	18.6
1980	67.8	80.9	14.6	19.1
1990	72.3	83.6	15.3	19.6

Source: Social Security Administration

Clearly people are living longer and many are healthier and able to do more later in life. This means that both your money and health has to last longer than previous generations. Many people also want to retire earlier than their parents. As a result people are spending more time in retirement than ever before.

The potential financial planning risks that our parents planned for are not necessarily those that we will face. The traditional concerns were market and investment risk – the risk of losing money in the market or to a poor investment. Now the largest risks that most people face are inflation and catastrophic medical expenses along with longevity.

It is vital to our quality of life that we plan based upon our own circumstances and goals not those of others or preconceived notions.

With our health planning each person is truly unique and their health plan should be as well. Even if 50 is the new 35 our bodies change as we age and what worked in the past may not work now. In some cases 35 may be the new 50. With the stress, extended work hours, poor eating habits, fast food, and enlarging waist lines we are placing our bodies in a significant compromised position that will break down sooner rather than later. We need to develop a plan based on where we truly are at today and based on where we want to go tomorrow.

We already know that we are a society of people who have made other things beside wellness and being fit their priorities. That situation is magnified greatly with the impact of aging. Frankly, we are all not that well prepared for growing old. We are actually pioneers in longevity!

The most important message to embrace is this: AGE SHOULD NOT BE A FACTOR ON HOW YOU LOOK OR FEEL!

Besides the obvious things we need to do to be healthy and fit what other considerations do we need to focus on in our later years? Statistics tells us we are going to live longer. Keep in mind, quantity of years going forward does not guarantee quality of life. We may have as many non-working years as we did working years. What are we going to do with them? Being healthy and fit with nothing to do can be as devastating as a chronic illness. So it's time to plan ahead and put some new behaviors in motion now to sustain you later.

> stop focusing on the age number

> Build strong relationships

> Active in your community whether it's a neighborhood, a building or a church

> Keeping social

> An active life of intimacy

> Learning new things

> Making friends

> Get enough sleep (7- 9 hours)

> Live in the moment

> Set goals for yourself

> Don't surround yourself with negative people

> Manage your sugar intake

> Eye and dental exams

> Eat good (non- processed) food and maintain a healthy weight

> Be careful to avoid falls: walk 3 times or more per week, at least 30 minutes

> Retain your medical records

> Embrace the concept of AGE Management and optimize your life

Age management is an individual plan, tailored to each person's health status. It focuses on prevention rather than treatment. This discipline is holistic in that it combines nutrition, lifestyle changes, supplements, exercise, stress management, hormonal balance and integrative medicine.

The goal is to maintain and optimize our mind and body functions so that they do not deteriorate over time. Usually we wait until it's too late and we cannot get the function back. Some people continue to believe there will be a quick fix, but the reality is that we are the only ones who can slow down the aging process and we have to be passionate and vigilant about it!

What to Expect & How to Manage

Your Key Health Systems	What's happening	What you can do	What you will do
Cardiovascular	• Hear rate slows, heart might be enlarged. • Blood vessels and arteries become stiff.	• Physical activity on a daily basis. Eat a healthy diet. • Do not smoke. • Manage stress.	
Bones, muscles and joints	• Bones experience shrinkage, and/or weakening. • Muscles lose strength & bulk. • Trouble with balance.	• Get adequate amounts of calcium, vitamin D. • Include physical activity in daily routine. • Avoid smoking Minimize alcohol exposure	
Digestive System	• Constipation	• Eat a healthy diet. • Include physical activity in your daily routine. • Drink plenty of water.	
Bladder and urinary tract	• Loss of bladder control and urinary tract health	• Go to bathroom regularly. • Maintain a healthy weight. • Don't smoke. • Do Kegel exercises.	
Endocrine Hormones	• Issues with cognition, mood, memory, sleep, energy, physical fitness, stamina, libido,	• Know your numbers. • Professional hormone optimization.	
Memory & Cognition	• Takes longer to learn new things or remember words or names	• Eat a healthy diet, with adequate brain nutrients. • Include physical activity in your daily routine • Stay mentally active • Be social	

As you can see, looking in the rearview mirror will NOT be an extension of what your forward looking years are for you. New challenges and hurdles will need to be faced head on to provide you with the strength of financial and physical health going forward. You need your own playbook since these customized chapters of your life are being written for the first time.

Chapter 5: The Action Plan

"A goal without a plan is just a wish" — Shibboleth

We all dream about achieving our personal goals and living our dreams and wishes. Far fewer take specific action to achieve those goals. What we do today will shape our future. We can all achieve our dreams but must take positive action. By reading this book and defining what is important to you, you have started on the road to achieving your vision.

To achieve your vision you need to take specific actions. Being motivated and doing the wrong things will just mean that you will do the wrong things faster and longer. As you plan you must have SMART goals - specific, measurable, applicable, relevant and with a defined time table. Your actions must be consistent with your true beliefs and values.

> Specific - goals must be very specific. For example, saying I want to lose weight is not specific - saying I want to lose 15 pounds is.

> Measurable - same as above - saying you will get in better shape is not measurable. Saying you will lower you cholesterol by 20% or lose 15 pounds is.

> Applicable - is the action and goal consistent with your compelling vision and dreams.

> Relevant - does the action or goal conflict with other goals? For example one goal may be to work. You have to decide what is most important and prioritize and eliminate the conflicts.

> Time - you must have a specific time frame for achieving the specific goal or action. For example saying you will lose 15lbs. is different than saying you will lose 15 lbs. in 5 months.

You must internalize and believe that the actions you take will help you achieve your dreams. Your goals should be positive - for example saying I want to lose 15 lbs. when you weigh 200 lbs. is different than "I WILL get to 185 lbs."

The entire process of achieving big dreams can be overwhelming. To make things more manageable you should break down your goals and actions by category and time-frame. You will also need to list a specific time frame for achieving these and the benefit/ reward you will have. You will look at immediate actions, 1 year, 3 year, 5 year, 10 year and 25 year plans. For each timeframe list your top three goals for the category plus any extra that you feel are important to make the list. Keep in mind, your goals over time can be a graduated process. This is not an overnight cram course for an examination that will come and go and be insignificant in the long run.

Your Immediate Plan:

Goal	Action Needed	Timeframe	Benefit
Health			
Financial			
Professional			
Personal/Spiritual			

Your One Year Plan:

Goal	Action Needed	Timeframe	Benefit
Health			
Financial			
Professional			
Personal/Spiritual			

Your Three Year Plan

Goal	Action Needed	Timeframe	Benefit
Health			
Financial			
Professional			
Personal/Spiritual			

Your Five Year Plan

Goal	Action Needed	Timeframe	Benefit
Health			
Financial			
Professional			
Personal/Spiritual			

Your 10 Year Plan

Goal	Action Needed	Timeframe	Benefit
Health			
Financial			
Professional			
Personal/Spiritual			

Your 25 Year Plan

Goal	Action Needed	Timeframe	Benefit
Health			
Financial			
Professional			
Personal/Spiritual			

There are several similarities between losing weight and building wealth. Most people understand the general concept of losing weight; you need to take in fewer calories than you burn. Yet, the majority of us are not successful in maintaining a healthy, let alone, athletic body. The same is true with building wealth. Most people understand that it is a matter of spending less than you earn; yet many are not successful at maintaining and/or enhancing their lifestyles over time.

There are three primary reasons that people are not successful with their weight loss or in building true wealth. The first is that many people simply do not have any idea of what to do or how to do it. The second is that even if we have a basic idea of what to do (burning calories or saving money) there really is more to being successful than may meets the eye. For example it's not just burning less calories than we take in, it is a matter of the types of calories (fats, proteins and carbohydrates) and building a plan that works for our individual body and lifestyle. Likewise, building wealth involves properly allocating between different types of asset classes (cash, fixed income, equities, etc.) and building a plan that makes sense for our personal goals, objectives and risk tolerance. Look at yourself as an orchestra conductor: a conductor of your own health and wealth, orchestrating all your financial and physical assets into beautiful symphony that is playing the music of your life!

This book is designed to help you develop a plan to meet your needs and goals. However, no book or program can make you execute and stay with your program. This is the third reason people are not successful with weight loss or building wealth; even if they have a plan they do not stick with it.

The concepts are not difficult but having the discipline to stick with your plan is not easy; or else everyone would be buff and wealthy! This book will give you the tools to maintain and enhance your life-style. It's up to you to be as successful as you want using the tools you are given. No one needs to do this on your own. You will need resources and advisors along the way! In Chapter 11 we discuss selecting advisors. So, complete the worksheets and let's continue our journey!

Chapter 6:
Modes of Change - Vehicles

Diet, exercise regimens and investments are all simply tools for achieving your vision. There are countless medications, nutritional supplements, investments and exercises. The combination that makes the most sense for you will depend upon your goals, needs, vision, risk tolerance, current health, time-frame and a number of other factors. There is no right or wrong answer. This is where a professional advisor can provide assistance. We have provided some basic and general information to serve as a basis for discussion with your advisors - not as a replacement for their knowledge and experience.

Successful people focus on their vision and utilize investments, nutritional supplements, exercises and medications to achieve this. Too often people focus on a particular investment or medication because they heard from a friend or advertisement that it is "good". Each persons situation is unique and therefore what is "good" for a friend may not make sense for you. Focus on your vision and then select the most appropriate tools for achieving it.

Very small changes today with regard to your health and financial planning will make a huge difference over time. Benefits are both cumulative and in many cases compound. Albert Einstein wrote:

"The most powerful force in the universe is compound interest"

This is because benefits – health, financial or any other – that compound grow exponentially. Consider if someone offered you the choice of a million dollars now or take a penny now and double the amount for 30 days. Most people would chose the million dollars now. But if you do the math a penny with the amount doubled every day for 30 days – 1 cent, then 2 cents, then 4 cents, then 8 cents, etc. grows to $5,368,709! The magic of compounding. Very small positive changes will make a huge difference over time in terms of your health, wealth and happiness. The sooner you start the sooner you will begin to benefit!

From an investment point of view there are several major types of investments that make up your portfolio. The allocation among these holdings (asset allocation) has been shown to be more important than the selection of the specific investments. In other words whether you pick fund A or fund B is far less important than if it is the right type of fund. From a health standpoint, you should be all inclusive, one body/ one mind, with an allocation of resources, looking at the whole and not the parts.

Put another way, if you are baking a cake the ratio of flour, sugar and baking powder is more important than the brand of each.

When developing an asset allocation the major categories of investments are:

1. Cash and equivalents

2. Fixed Income- both foreign and domestic

3. Equities- both foreign and domestic

4. Alternative Investments and Hard Assets

Your specific allocation should be based upon your situation not what you feel the markets or economy are doing. The allocation should be based upon your current and future income needs, risk tolerance, tax situation and long term goals to name a few. It is important to have different asset types and classes to offset the various types of risks that we face (we discuss this more in Chapter 10). An an asset that helps protect from one type of risk may expose you to another. For example cash has very little market risk but it generally does not keep up with inflation. Equities fluctuate in value but will generally keep up and exceed inflation. By having some of each asset class you can balance risk with your needs.

Generally your asset allocation should include some of all four of the above. How much of each will depend upon you. Your professional financial advisor can assist in developing an asset allocation that meets your needs, objectives and risk tolerance.

Once established it is critical that you monitor the allocation and then update your portfolio based upon changes to markets, interest rates, tax law and your situation. We recommend reviewing and updating every three to six months depending on your situation and not less than twice per year.

In our opinion any investment program, or health regimine that takes more than 5 minutes to understand is probably too complicated. With regard to investments we recommend against anything that ties you up with potential penalties if a change is needed or that charge a large up front fee.

Your philosophical approach to both health care and financial planning is critical to your overall health management and invest-ment strategy. Do you believe in "sick" care or "health"care. There is a big difference and the difference is you and your commitment to the end goal.

When it comes to your health, it's time to view your investment from a new perspective. For example, if you generally see your doc-tor only when you are sick and the over the counter remedies don't work, then you are in a reactive health mode. If you think that the only health care worth getting is what is covered by your health in-surance plan then you are not committed to managing your assets, your most important assets, to achieve your personal best health.

The first step toward changing your perspective is in selecting a physician to be your partner in this process. The next step is in de-veloping a working relationship with your doctor which comes over time with mutual trust. The heart of this process is knowing what your goal is and working with the doctor to achieve it. That means doing the things you both agreed upon and staying the course. It means being honest with the doctor and yourself.

What you really need is a Wellness Partner/Coach and your goals should be achieving your best health, your best nutrition, your best exercise plan and ultimately your best life!

How do you find and select a physician to work with you?

1. Check your insurance company's website for providers in your area,

2. Ask friends/coworkers/family/etc. who they go to,

3. Or, ask in person by setting up an introductory visit with a physician,

    And consider, asking over social media if you're not shy.

4. Search for physicians on the internet by typing your issue and area code (i.e. metabolic syndrome, 89123) or by typing in the type of doctor you'd like and area code (i.e. endocrinologist, 89123)

5. Search for physicians on hospital websites. Most hospital websites will have a search page that allows patients to search for physicians that are associated with the hospital.

6. Research the physician on the internet once you have a name:

    >   Look up the physician on the state medical board's website to make sure no complaints have been lodged, see what specialties they listed for their licenses, see what medical school they went to and when the graduated,

    >   Look up the physician on sites like Yelp to see patient reviews,

    >   Visit the physician's website (if there is one),

    >   Search for the physician on the internet to see if they've written any articles/been involved with any projects.

7. When in doubt, call the office to see if the physician treats your issue.

   > If they don't, ask if they have any recommendations on physicians that can treat your issue.

8. In some cases you will need to assemble a team of health care providers to cover all your bases. It will be worth it to have the right players on your team!

Identify your health goals and validate them with your health care team. Together you can build a step by step plan to achieve your goals.

Finding a good financial advisor is much like finding a good health care provider/advisor. What you really need is a true partner who understands your personal goals, objectives and risk tolerance. There are many qualified financial advisors and physicians – the key is finding someone who you feel comfortable with and listens to you. Moreover, is their approach to financial planning or healthcare consistent with what YOU are seeking?

How do you find and select a financial advisor to work with you? We will discuss different types of advisors in Chapter11. Once you know think about who you would like to work with:

1. Ask friends/coworkers/family/etc. who they go to,

2. Search the internet using key phrases considtent with what you are seeking.

3. Consider, asking over social media if you're not shy

First and foremost you should feel comfortable with the advisors you select. Go and speak to several different folks and see who "clicks". You can then check credentials and compliance history for any securities licensed advisors and/or their firms via finra.org broker check.

Finally for those of you who have gone great lengths to find the right hair dresser, the best golf pro and the right car deal: You know who you are! Consider taking as much time and putting in the same effort to find the right health care and wealth planning team for yourself!

Chapter 7:
Protecting Your Greatest Asset

Have you ever asked yourself this question, "What is my most valuable asset?" Would the response differ if it was answered by your Child, Doctor, Teacher, Psychologist, Clergy or Financial Advisor? Peel away the layers and look deep inside yourself. What is really YOUR most valuable asset? The greatest asset is YOU! Now that you are getting a clearer picture about the answer, do you believe in it, respect it, honor it, take care of it and OWN IT? In the following chapter we would like to share with you our experience with working with people and how they regard their asset(s).

When I see a patient for the first time, the book is open and new chapters are ready to be composed. Usually whatever operating system one has worked with either needs an upgrade or a new software change. Going through the twists and turns of life can draw on our physical energy, constrict our emotional expression, wear down our mental capacity and what does one have left...a hollow asset with limited operating capacity. Recognizing and protecting this asset requires attention on a daily basis to run the full course of life with optimum functioning and efficiency. Obtaining optimal physical, mental, emotional and spiritual health is a balance of all parts. Some weigh heavier than others depending on the time and circumstances. Each part requires essential ingredients for it to function well. Neglecting or ignoring the essentials will manifest at some point and result in dysfunctional imbalances. We are responsible for who we are and what we do with ourselves. Essential ingredients of health require proper healthy nutrition to fuel our system, wholesome relationships with our family, friends, coworkers and all those we come in touch within our lives. Our physical body requires movement and exercise that is part of us and not just another Task dictated to us. As we understand what the totality of life is about and follow what one can learn from reading, instruction and most of all having an advisor who can respect your assets and illuminate the path of good health, then you are on your way.

During my first encounter with a patient, a question that I often ask goes like this, "If I were your healthcare genie and could grant you 3 wishes (pertaining to health) that could be resolved and help you move forward what would that be?" What do you think are the most common responses I encounter? In no specific order, here are the common ones: "I want more energy, I want to feel better, I want to lose weight, I want my sex drive back, I want to stop losing my hair, I want a better life". These wishes can be fulfilled when securing the foundation of health with the very basic necessities of life. This is not putting a band aid over a dysfunctional part but getting to the source of generator of the problem and fixing it. You are not alone and it is never hopeless.

Aside from the intangible assets that we all behold, our life is also rounded out by the non-personal assets that also help shape the lifestyle that gives flavor to life's enjoyment. Building the treasure chest of these assets can take a lifetime of work, dedication and discipline, but it's never too late to start. Just as one values the quality of health and life one also needs to respect the importance of a solid secure financial base. Just as you might research a Doctor you would trust with your health, you also need to take the same course of investigation for a financial advisor you would trust with your wealth.

Approaching a client pertaining to their lifestyle and wealth aspirations is no different from the first patient encounter above. When people are asked by a financial advisor what their most valuable asset is, most respond that their house, car, retirement plan or business is most valuable. From a financial advisor perspective, your greatest most valuable asset is your ability to maintain and enhance your standard of living. An essential financial ingredient is INCOME. For people who are not yet retired this is your ability to earn income. Most people protect their car, house, and other possessions, but neglect to protect the most valuable asset they own: their power to generate income and to protect their wealth.

The extent of the risk of a serious injury or illness affecting your ability to earn a living is startling. The probability of a 35 year old being disabled for more than three months before age 65 is over 50%. People in their 40s are three times more likely to be disabled than die before age 65. And the numbers get worse as you get older for remaining disabled for 5 years or more. Yet a great majority of the population has no disability coverage beyond Social Security and worker's compensation.

To evaluate your disability income needs, begin with an estimate of the income that will be needed during disability. Once the income need has been established, the resources available should be deducted. The first deduction should be from any employer paid short-term disability or group insurance benefits. Next, you may wish to consider social security disability benefits. However, the social security system rejects most of the claims made for disability benefits. Finally, reduce the monthly income need by earnings from other sources such as interest and dividends on investments. The remaining balance is the disability insurance need. You should note that insurance companies limit the amount of income they will replace through a disability benefit, so you may not be able to insure the entire need.

As you might expect, the key to any disability insurance policy is its definition of the term "disabled." There are four key definitions of disability: "any occupation," "own occupation," "reduction in income," and "residual." You are disabled under an "any occupation" definition when your condition prevents you from doing anything for anybody that will bring home a paycheck. It is the most restrictive definition.

The "own occupation" definition is far more favorable. Under this definition you are disabled if your condition prevents you from performing the major duties of your occupation. For example, under an "own occupation" policy, a heart surgeon is still disabled even if he could work as a professor of medicine. The precise language of "own occupation" policies varies from insurer to insurer, so it pays to read these policies carefully.

"Income reduction" is a relatively recent innovation. Under these policies, you are disabled as long as your condition forces you to earn less than you were earning before you were sick or injured. How much less you have to earn depends on the policy.

"Residual disability" is also a recent innovation. This definition is an enhancement of an "own occupation" policy. Frequently, a person's disability may permit them to return to their own occupation, but only at "half speed." In other words, it may take a considerable period of time after they return to work to get back to their former level of earnings. The "residual disability" provision is designed to provide benefits to bridge that gap.

As a physician, I cannot emphasize enough the importance of the plan that fits your life circumstances. It is a critical first step to protect you financially. The right choice of plan will be one less hurdle you will have to deal with if ever it needs to be executed. As a Neurologist, I have seen how important the right match for the individual can be a game changer if the unfortunate unpredictable health circumstance falls upon one.

As one approaches retirement you will want to consider Long Term Care insurance which is outlined in the following appendix. You are protecting not only the financial availability of care for yourself but also protecting your assets from years of savings which will vaporize in a short span of time due to the exorbitant cost of care that only a very few can sustain.

Of course, this brief chapter is no substitute for a careful consideration of all of the advantages and disadvantages of this matter in light of your unique personal circumstances. Before implementing any significant tax or financial planning strategy, contact your financial planner, attorney or tax advisor as appropriate.

Chapter 8:
How Much Do I Need? Key Benchmarks

How much money do I need to retire? What should my blood pressure and cholesterol numbers be? Benchmarks are objective numbers that help us to judge where we are and how we are doing. The key is to select benchmarks that are appropriate for our personal situation. In this case the medical numbers are more easily defined versus financial. We have included tables for height, weight, pulse and blood pressure for your reference with the caveat that we have to understand what these numbers really mean and how they relate to our situation. For example an average person who is 5 feet 6 inches tall will weigh "X" on a reference chart but a body builder may be perfectly healthy with a very low body fat and weigh 250 lbs. That does not mean it is OK for you to weigh 250 pounds!

How much money do you need to retire? The answer, like so many other things, is that it depends. This depends on how much income you need to live the way you want and also how long you will need the income. Once we have an idea of how much will be needed we can determine what needs to be saved to achieve our goal.

How long will my savings last in retirement? This depends on both your asset allocation and market conditions at the time withdrawals are being made. For years, the rule-of-thumb answer has been 4 percent, adjusted annually for inflation. But a growing number of financial planning experts are re-thinking that number. The Four Percent Rule stems from financial planning research done in the

1990s by William Bengen (1994 article in the Journal of Financial Planning on sustainable rates) and a subsequent influential study by three researchers at Trinity University.

New research suggests that an initial 4 percent withdrawal rate may be high and a 3% (adjusted for inflation) withdrawal rate is more reasonable. Studies have shown that a 4% withdrawal rate leads to only a 50 percent probability of success over a 30-year period for a balanced portfolio. For a portfolio containing 40 percent equities, boosting the odds of success to 90 percent requires reducing the initial withdrawal rate to 2.8 percent. Determining the appropriate withdrawal rate from a portfolio to cover your expenses is a challenging but important exercise.

In our opinion a good rule of thumb for planning is that a 3% withdrawal rate will be sustainable for an extended period form a well-diversified portfolio which includes equities, fixed income and cash. One of the mistakes people make is thinking that certain investments are "safe" because they are not in the market when they actually have different types of risks such as from inflation (See Chapter 10 for more information in this regard).

In a number of studies W.P Bengen found that a retirement portfolio with a 50% equity-50% long-term bond allocation is able to sustain a 3% inflation-adjusted withdrawal rate for any possible 30-year period starting in 1926 and through 1996. After examining alternative asset allocations and withdrawal rates, Bengen concluded that if the market behaves in the future the way it has in the past, of which there is no guarantee, then the typical retirement fund should have a 50-75% equity allocation, which would allow a 4% inflation adjusted withdrawal rate for 35 years. More recent studies suggest that a portfolio with 50% - 60% in equities will have a reasonable probability of generating a 3% (inflation adjusted withdrawal rate) for 30 years.

So to figure out how much you need to have in retirement, and how much we should be saving, we first need to determine what our anticipated income need will be. Once we have that we can figure out how much of a portfolio we need to generate the income based on a 3% withdrawal rate.

For example if we determine that we need to generate $25,000 per year then we divide this by 3% to find out the amount we need in our retirement savings - $25,000/3% = $833,333.

We can then determine how much we need to be saving today to have this amount in the future. The amount we need to save will depend on what rate of return we can earn on our savings. For example if we need $833,000 25 years from now we would need to save $13,175 per year if we could earn 7% but would need to save $22,856 if we are earning 3%.

Your professional financial advisor can help you determine what your current and future needs are and what you need to save to have a reasonable probably of achieving your retirement income needs and wishes. There are also a number of online resources for calculating retirement savings needs and potential income.

In planning for the future you should also familiarize yourself with the potential future challenges for your personal health .

The real message here is to start your preventive plan now to ward off the impact of aging and prepare your body to fight of illness. Think about the power of the compounding penny! The details of the plan for you needs to be developed with your wellness team and it will be customized to you, just like your long term financial plan will be geared to your situation.

Bengen, W. P. (1994). Determining withdrawal rates using historical data. Journal of Financial Planning, 7(1),171-180.

Bengen, W. P. (1996). Asset allocation for a lifetime. Journal of Financial Planning, 9(3), 58-67.

Bengen, W. P. (1997). Conserving client portfolio during retirement, part III. Journal of Financial Planning,10(5), 84-97.

Bierwirth, L. (1994). Investing for retirement: using the past to model the future. Journal of Financial Planning, 7(1), 14-24.

Chapter 9: The Decisions We Make

Decisions that we make regarding our health care, financial planning and a myriad of other things are based on a number of factors. We rely upon our experience, our expectations and our needs. Biases in judgment and decision making have been demonstrated by research in psychology and behavioral economics. These are systematic deviations from a standard of what would otherwise be considered rational or good judgment.

The reality of these biases is confirmed by replicable research, however, there are controversies about how to explain these biases Some are effects of information-processing rules, called heuristics that the brain uses to produce decisions or judgments. These are called cognitive biases. Biases in judgment or decision-making can also result from motivation such as when beliefs are distorted by wishful thinking. Some biases have a variety of cognitive ("cold") or motivational ("hot") explanations. Both effects can be present at the same time.

When decisions are based on the cost it is called behavioral finance. Behavioral finance is a fancy way to describe how and why we make decisions based on financial considerations.

When it comes to health care, the financial decision -making process often precedes the medical decision. People will put off going to the doctor because it's inconvenient, they might miss work, they don't want to pay for the office visit or even a copay.

People will choose to feel lousy and tough it out before they will spend the money on getting care. They generally wait until the situation is critical and it ends up taking longer and costing more than if they had just gotten the attention they needed immediately.

Do you ask yourself these questions?

> > Is it covered by insurance?

> > Can I get that RX in generic?

> > Do I really need this test? How much is it?

They are not bad questions on their own but when they become excuses not to invest in your own care then they are barriers to your long term wellness.

Getting to the root cause of an illness is just as important as the treatment. We can then determine how to prevent the situation in the future and identify any other mitigating factors that could impact your overall health.

Mowing the lawn and cutting down the flower or leaf at the stem of a weed will not stop the offending plant from returning. You need to burrow down into the earth and eradicate the whole plant in order to kill it off completely, otherwise it will reappear. Cutting it will likely slow down its growth, but that's all. This is the same concept with dealing with physical illness and energetic imbalances, treating the "showy" symptoms is not enough. We must dig deeper, discover the cause, and treat the root issue in order to bring about a complete healing. Depending on how deep a root cause is, healing can take a while. It may take months or years, and in some cases, a lifetime. Just remember, healing is a journey.

It is actually best to treat imbalances in the early stages before they have had the opportunity to take root and manifest into the physical body. For example in the case of hereditary diseases, taking life style precautions (i.e. healthy diet, regular exercise) is an appropriate preventative measure.

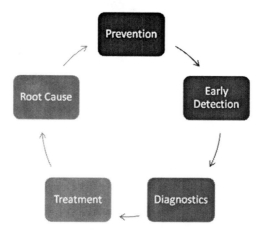

With regard to our investments the decision should be much easier. While cost should always be a consideration the amount of return that we net after any fee's or expense is the most important consideration. For example if we have one investment that has a 1% expense and pays us 5% and another that has a 3% expense that pays us (net) 10% then clearly the second one is better. Ultimately, as with medical tests or procedures, the bigger question is whether or not a particular investment will help us achieve our personal goals.

Whether or not to have a medical test or procedure or to make an investment should be based upon your specific needs, objectives and vision.

1. Dougherty, M. R. P., Gettys, C. F., & Ogden, E. E. (1999). MINERVA-DM: A memory processes model for judgments of likelihood. Psychological Review, 106(1), 180–209

2. Kahneman, D.; Tversky, A. (1972), "Subjective probability: A judgment of representativeness", Cognitive Psychology 3: 430–454, doi:10.1016/0010-0285(72)90016-3.

3. Baron, J. (2007). Thinking and deciding (4th ed.). New York, NY: Cambridge University Press

Chapter 10: Road Hazards

As we proceed on our journey we will inevitably face some impediments along the way. There are those we see and those that may not really be a hazard at all. It is often the bus we don't see coming – not the one we do – that hits us. So too is the case with our health and financial planning. It is critical to understand the real risks that we face and then make decisions which help us achieve our personal vision. Often there are misperceptions and misunderstanding of what the real risks we face because of the popular media or preconceived notions. As with other aspects of our planning the risks we face are not necessarily those of our parents or others.

One of the mistakes that people make with both their health and finances is to make changes after there is a problem. With investments people want to sell high and buy low but often do the opposite for a number of reasons – some of which are outlined below. The key is to be proactive in your financial and health planning rather than reacting to problems. Having a real understanding of potential risks we face will help us proactively make adjustments. Moreover, by decreasing one risk you may inadvertently increase another. For example taking a medication to help with one problem could have a negative interaction with another you are taking for a different problem making the entire situation worse not better. With investments there is often trade off between different risks that needs to balanced based upon your needs, objectives, tax situation and risk tolerance. Identifying that potential issues will impact you and how to mitigate these based upon your goals is another area that your professional health care and financial advisor can assist.

Some of the financial risks that we face are:

> Investment risk – the risk that an investment does poorly. By properly diversifying the portfolio we can minimize this type of risk. We don't want all of our eggs in one basket so to speak.

> Inflation risk – the risk that we will not be able to maintain our standard of living in the future due to inflation. We need to invest our money to grow at a rate faster than inflation and taxes reduce our buying power. Generally, equity type investments will be the only things to do this. Many people don't think about inflation risk as they focus more on investment risk. Yet with life expectancies increasing this is one of the major risks that most people face.

> Interest rate risk – As interest rates rise, bond prices fall and vice versa. The rationale is that as interest rates increase, the value of the investment decreases since investors are able to realize greater yields by switching to other investments that reflect the higher interest rate

> Reinvestment risk is the chance that an investor won't be able to reinvest cash flows from an investment at a rate equal to the investment's current rate of return.

For example, consider a Company XYZ bond with a 10% yield to maturity. In order for an investor to actually receive the expected yield to maturity, she must reinvest the interest payments she receives at a 10% rate. This is not always possible. If the investor could only reinvest at 4% (say, because market returns fell after the bonds were issued), the investor's actual return on the bond would be lower than expected.

> Excessive withdrawals: As discussed in Chapter 8. Taking more than 3% - 4% on a well balanced portfolio may deplete principal over time.

> Catastrophic Medical Expense – There are several types of potential medical expenses both while working and once retired to consider. First is insuring your income. Your ability to earn money may be your most valuable asset prior to retirement. You will want to insure against both medical expenses and a possible disability that would not allow you to earn. It is important to insure against medical expenses and also the potential cost of Long Term Care. Long Term Care expense is one of the largest unfunded liabilities Americans face today and you should purchase your policy at age 45-50, when you are in your best physical health in the last half of your life.

    See Appendix: Disability Insurance – insuring your most valuable asset

                                   Long Term Care insurance

                                   Medical Insurance

> Fear & Greed – Often individuals become fearful when they see their portfolio drop in value and conversely become greedy when they hear about the latest and greatest way

to make money. In a study by Dalbar Inc. from 1985 to 2004 the average mutual fund investor achieved a 3.7% annualized return while the S&P500 achieved a return of 11.9% and inflation averaged 3%. The Dalbar Inc. study found that the reason for the average mutual fund investor's low return was that these investors invested more in "Hot Performing" mutual funds at the end of bull markets and then became frightened and took money out of the market toward the end of bear markets.

The average fixed income investor earned 4.24% annually; compared to the long-term government bond index of 11.70%. (source: Dalbar)

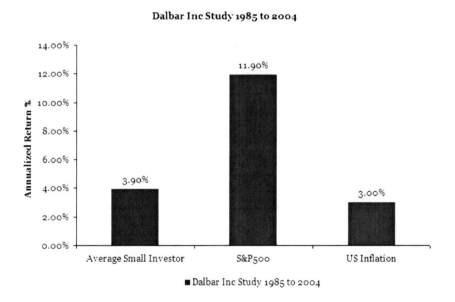

Dalbar Inc Study 1985 to 2004

Chasing the latest craze does not make sense for a long term investor and is a side trip that will divert you from your long term path to success. Moreover, trying to time the market may increase transaction and tax cost.

The Risk of Market Timing

Trying to pick the right time to get in and out of the market may increase portfolio risk significantly. The chart below shows that missing the best ten months since 1980 would have cost you more than $180,000 on a $10,000 investment and missing just the 20 best months – out of 372 cost you more than $240,000 on a $10,000 investment. It is human nature to get fearful when markets drop and greedy when they start to move up- but trying to time the markets is one of the biggest mistakes one can make. You need to have an asset allocation that is based on your needs, objectives and risk tolerance – not day to day or even year to year market swings or predictions. Changes to the allocation should be made based upon our needs and goals not fear, greed or specula- tion. Yes this is the same issue we discussed above but is also one of the most common mistakes people make!

Return on a lump sum investment of $10,000 invested in the S&P 500 Index		
January 1, 1980 – December 31, 2011	Return	Ending Value of $10,000 investment
Staying invested for the full period	11.06%	$286,700
Missing the 5 best months	9.12%	$163,290
Missing the 10 best months	7.49%	$100,770
Missing the 15 best months	6.09%	$66,248
Missing the 20 best months	4.83%	$45,284

This is a hypothetical example used for illustrative purposes only. The return figures are based on a hypothetical $10,000 investment in the S&P 500 Index from January 1, 1980 - December 31, 2011. The lump sum investment in common stocks would have reflected the same stocks/weightings as represented in the S&P 500 Index. The example does not represent or project the actual performance of any security, or other investment product. The hypothetical figures do not reflect the impact of any commissions, fees or taxes applicable to an actual investment. The S&P 500®Index is an unmanaged, market capitalization-weighted index of 500 widely held U.S. stocks recognized by investors to be representative of the stock market in general. It is provided to represent the investment environment existing for the time period shown. The returns shown do not reflect the actual cost of investing in the instruments that comprise it. You cannot invest in an index. Standard & Poor's and S&P 500 are trademarks of the McGraw-Hill Companies, Inc. the Best 10 Months

Having too much Corporate Stock- We all want to believe in our company and often whether public or private we invest. Regardless of the investment it is important not to become overly concentrated in any single investment due to investment risk.

Finally a big risk is not understanding risk. This is true for financial planning, health planning and all other aspects of life. For example many people feel that a bank account or certificate of deposit is "safe" and by that they mean it will not fluctuate. The risk with these types of investments is from inflation and perhaps also income tax and interest rates. Different asset types (stocks, bonds, bank accounts, etc.) will have different types of risk. Generally the more potential return something offers the more volatile or illiquid it will be – that is why it pays a higher return. The key is to properly diversify your portfolio so that it meets your risk tolerance, personal goals and objectives. A trained professional (Financial, Medical, Legal, Tax, etc.) in the area you are working can help to identify, quantify and mitigate the risks that you really face.

Health Care Hazards and Risks

There is one major hazard or risk: it is your current lifestyle! You can improve your lifestyle in three steps:

Overcoming the risks:

1. Do not smoke, drink excessively or do illegal drugs

2. Be physically active

3. Eat well

Insuring Your Health: Insurance for health is undergoing a renaissance of change. As you are aware the change rarely puts you first. When considering your plan you should have the mindset that insurance is a back stop against major catastrophic loss. People get hung up on copays and the bells and whistles of health plans. When searching for what would make sense for you, consider the following calculations.

What were your total health care premiums paid out of pocket per year for the last 3 years?

_____

_____

Did you meet your deductible and was it to your advantage from a cost savings standpoint?

_____

Calculate costs for a higher deductible with potential savings in a health savings account (HSA) when using pre-tax dollars placed away for future sick care.

Common Health Misconceptions: Changing lab numbers rarely reflect how you really feel. How often have you heard "your numbers look great", but you still feel terrible? Consider this a big, flashing, warning sign. You feel terrible because you are not right and you know it. This is where you need your Wellness Team!

Annual Physical Exam: Once a year is not enough to maintain good health. Our bodies are the most dynamic piece of biology on the planet. Do you really think proper monitoring and adjustments can be done once a year? Visits with your wellness team 2-3 times a year keeps one on track to achieve optimal health.

Nutritional Supplements: In the age we live and the food that is grown from depleted nutrient soil is not the same nutritionally dense food that our grandparents consumed. Toxic exposures to pesticides, herbicides, drug residues in our water supply and polluted animal products place an excess burden on our systems to handle. We face endocrine disrupters resulting in mind and behavior challenges, weight gain, low energy and reduced immunity which can lead to major health issues. You must supply adequate nutrients to your body to fuel the necessary processes of your life systems.

TV Consultants: You cannot have your health needs customized and tailored for you by watching daytime health talk shows. Introduction to the basics is good. However, if you design a program with all the touted TV tips, never fail, you will end up with a closet of full of pills that provide you with little noticeable change, except for the absolute reduction of your own cash.

Chapter 11: Selecting Advisors

With both your medical and financial planning the outcome will be largely dependent upon the advisors you select to help you. When selecting an advisor at the very least you need to verify their professional credentials and their areas of specialization. You would not go to a cardiologist for a broken hip. Beyond that it is critical to work with someone who is passionate about what they do and who will take the time to learn what your goals and vision are. There are a lot of technically competent professionals who are too busy or too overworked to spend the time needed to really learn about you. As with all successful relationships you should feel good about communicating with your advisor and feel that they really "get you" and understand your vision.

Before the internet one issue of handling your own financial and medical matters was a lack of information. Today the internet is full of information – the issue is sorting through it all and deciding what is relevant, accurate and necessary. It is somewhat like trying to drink from a fire hose! Moreover, much of what is touted as fact is incomplete, inaccurate or just wrong. Even with good information the key is applying it to your situation.

Once you have decided where you need or want to go you then need to decide how to get there. The route you are going to take and the vehicles that you will use. Generally there are a number choices with regard to both. The choices that you make will depend upon a number of things including, but not limited to, your budget, your specific needs, your goals and your advisor. Hiring a good advisor will make all the difference on your journey and it's outcome.

Just like deciding to hire a travel agent for your trip the first step is to decide to hire a financial and medical advisor rather than doing it yourself. Once you have decided to do so – and for most people a good advisor will help you achieve your long term goals and objectives more easily than going it alone – then you need to decide what type of advisor(s) to hire. Ultimately you will want to build a team of health care, financial, tax and legal advisors to help you in your journey.

Your Financial Team

We need to differentiate among different types of advisors and services. There are many people who call themselves financial advisors or planners. The following is a brief guide.

Even if you have the time and the desire to manage your own money hiring a professional advisor or advisors can give you an independent perspective, expertise and help manage expectations. Moreover, they may be aware of investment products and services or the nuances of investments which you are not. Besides do you want to spend time doing financial planning or enjoying your life?

The following is a partial list of people who provide financial services and or advice. Just like seeking out a medical professional you first need to decide what type of professional you need (doctor, dentist, nurse, specialist, surgeon, etc.) and then you need to decide who to go to. The next chapter discussed how to select an advisor.

Registered Representative/Stock Brokers

A Registered Representative, also called a General Securities Representative, a Stock Broker, or an Account Executive, is an individual who is licensed to sell securities. Registered Representatives usually work for broker-dealers licensed by the Securities Exchange Commission (SEC) and the Self Regulatory Organization (SRO) known as the Financial Industry Regulatory Authority (FINRA). To become a Registered Representative, one must be sponsored by a broker-dealer firm and pass the FINRA-administered Series 7 examination or another Limited Representative Qualifications Exam. Some state laws and broker-dealer policies require the Series 63 examination to be passed, as well.

Financial Planner – this is a generic term that anyone can use. To be a Certified Financial Planner CFP® the individual must undergo a rigorous course and examination. Often stock brokers, insurance agents and others who are not CFPs hold themselves out as financial planners. A financial planner may or may not be securities licensed (series 7).

Insurance Agent – the representative for an insurer. He may be an independent agent representing the products of a collection of insurance companies, or he may be a dedicated agent who represents a single company. Some agents specialize in selling certain kinds of policies such as life insurance, or annuities sold to individuals, or various kinds of insurance sold to small businesses or corporations. An agent usually works for an agency. The types of licenses that an agent holds will depend upon the state they work in and the types of insurance they sell. An insurance agent may also hold specialized designations such as CLU – certified life underwriter or ChFC Charter

The CLU is a professional designation for individuals who specialize in life insurance and estate planning. Individuals must complete five core courses and three elective courses, and successfully pass all eight two-hour, 100-question examinations in order to receive the designation.

The ChFC is a financial planning designation for the insurance industry awarded by the American College of Bryn Mawr. ChFCs must meet experience requirements and pass exams covering finance and investing. They must have at least three years of experience in the financial industry, and have studied and passed an examination on the fundamentals of financial planning, including income tax, insurance, investment and estate planning.

Registered Investment Advisor (RIA) - is someone generally paid a fee for advice but who is not a securities broker (no series 7). An RIA advisor or firm is engaged in the investment advisory business and registered either with the Securities and Exchange Commission (SEC) or state securities authorities. A Registered Investment Advisor is defined by The Investment Advisers Act of 1940 as a "person or firm that, for compensation, is engaged in the act of providing advice, making recommendations, issuing reports or furnishing analyses on securities, either directly or through publications." An investment advisor has a fiduciary duty to his or her clients, which means that he or she has a fundamental obligation to provide suitable investment advice and always act in the clients' best interests. This is considered a higher standard than that of a regular registered rep or broker.

When it comes to compensation, advisors fall into four categories:

1. Salary based - You pay the company for which the advisor works, and the company pays its advisors a salary.

2. Fee based - You pay a fee based on an hourly rate (for specific advice or a financial plan), or based on a percentage of your assets and/or income. A fee based on assets is becoming a more common approach as it helps align your interest with that of the advisor.

3. Commission based--The advisor receives a commission from a third party for any products you may purchase. Often times the commission is included in the price of the product so it is important to discuss this with your advisor and or review a prospectus for any security which outlines fees and expenses

4. Commission and fee based--The advisor receives a combination or choice of commissions and fee compensation

You'll need to decide which type of compensation structure works best for you, based on your own personal circumstances and what your advisor recommends. The key is understanding what the expense is and getting true value. The least expensive financial advisor may not be the best one for you any more than the least expensive health care provider.

Finally you will want to consider how your tax, legal and investment advisors will work together for your benefit. Often the financial planner will coordinate efforts to avoid redundancy and help create a cohesive plan for you.

Your Medical Team

Finding your way around the medical maze can be quite challenging. New roles have been assumed and directed whether it be by insurance companies, institutions or offices. You are caught in the middle and trying to figure out the Who's Who of Your Health. The following are some definitions that may help you understand who does what.

A Nurse Practitioner (NP) is an advanced practice registered nurse (APRN) who has completed additional Nurse practitioners training to treat both physical and mental conditions through comprehensive history taking, physical exams, and ordering tests for interpretation. NPs can provide a diagnosis and recommendations for a wide range of acute and chronic diseases (within their scope of practice) and provide appropriate treatment for patients, including prescribing medications in some states. NPs can serve as a patient's primary health care provider, and see patients of all ages depending on their specialty (family, pediatrics, geriatrics, etc.).

A Physican Assistant (PA), is a healthcare professional who is trained to practice medicine as part of a team with physicians. Physician assistants are concerned with preventing and treating human illness and injury by providing a broad range of health care services under the direction of a physician or surgeon. Physician assistants conduct physical exams, diagnose and treat illnesses, order and interpret tests, prescribe medications, counsel on preventive health care and may assist in surgery

Family Medicine, formerly Family Practice (FP), is a medical specialty devoted to comprehensive health care for people of all ages; the specialist is named a family physician, family doctor, or formerly family practitioner. It is a division of primary care that provides continuing and comprehensive health care for the individual and family across all ages, genders, diseases, and parts of the body. It is based on knowledge of the patient in the context of the family and the community, emphasizing disease prevention and patient care. In addition to diagnosing and treating illness, they also provide preventive care, including routine checkups, health-risk assessments, immunization and screening tests, and personalized counseling on maintaining a healthy lifestyle.

Integrative Wellness Physicians/Holistic Medicine

Holistic medicine is a form of healing that considers the whole person -- body, mind, spirit, and emotions -- in the quest for optimal health and wellness. According to the holistic medicine philosophy, one can achieve optimal health -- the primary goal of holistic medicine practice -- by gaining proper balance in life. Holistic medicine practitioners believe that the whole person is made up of interdependent parts and if one part is not working properly, all the other parts will be affected. In this way, if people have imbalances (physical, emotional, or spiritual) in their lives, it can negatively affect their overall health. A holistic doctor may use all forms of health care, from conventional medication to alternative therapies, to treat a patient. Complementary and alternative therapies such as acupuncture, chiropractic care, homeopathy, massage therapy, naturopathy, and others.

Holistic providers may include medical doctors, doctors of osteopathy, naturopathic doctors, chiropractors, and homeopathic doctors. To find a holistic practitioner in your area, visit the American Holistic Medical Association web site. There you can use an online provider search to find a practitioner near you.

Anti-aging/ Regenerative Medicine Specialist: The specialist in this area is an MD or DO by training and board certification in a medicine/osteopathic subspecialty. Requirements for board certification include oral and written board examination through the American Board of Anti Aging and Regenerative Medicine. There is fellowship training in areas of nutritional based medicine, bioidentical hormone therapy, and approach to medical conditions using a holistic natural based approach to support the body in healing.

Nutritionist: is a person who advises on matters of food and nutrition impacts on health. Different professional terms are used in different countries, employment settings and contexts — some examples include: nutrition scientist, public health nutritionist, dietitian-nutritionist, clinical nutritionist, and sports nutritionist.

Dietitians are experts in food and nutrition ("dietetics"). They advise people on what to eat in order to lead a healthy lifestyle or achieve a specific health-related goal. Dietitians work in various capacities in the field of healthcare, foodservice, corporate setting, and educational arenas

Chapter 12: Your Health

Health can be defined in many different ways. How does one get to good or excellent health? Many volumes of books have been written on health. The real question for YOU is "how do I optimize ME"?

As you will come to realize there are many paths that can lead to "DH", Destination Health. For some, one path will suffice. However, for many one path is not sufficient to reach that all-encompassing destination of prime health. You will know when you are there because you will feel a sense of completeness, a pinnacle of physical, mental and psychological health, a sense of total wholeness. Once you are there, you will be open to living life experiences totally unencumbered.

The paths outlined here are optional for some and mandatory for others depending on their situation. Conventional medical care is a path frequently traveled at this time and in the age we live at present. For some it is the only path traveled. No judgment on wrong or right, just what one may choose. For many it is the only path known to them. Feeder paths may tie in with some and others may run parallel but not always exclusive.

As one looks at the physical body, we realize that as we age our body is ever changing and not always for the better. We have challenges of brain function decline, musculoskeletal decline, organ system decline, and an outward appearance of the changes of aging.

Foundational health, core pillars of our physical existence include hormone optimization and nutritional health. Meeting these basic tenets will provide one with the essence of combating modern day challenges. Natural based hormones whether produced by our bodies or supplemented to obtain normal levels are one of the keys to best gene expression to produce the best biochemistry our body has to offer. This is not exclusive to the needs of adequate nutrition or the right food substances which provide the energy source needed by the cells of our body, organs and system of the body to function with robust balance.

Treatment of hormone imbalance or decline with bioidentical or natural based hormones can be life direction changing for many who pursue this path. Balancing of major league hormones including thyroid, cortisol, testosterone, estrogen, progesterone and DHEA will impact many bodily systems simultaneously leading to a symphony score of health. Properly trained physicians understanding the science and how the body works are ever growing in number. The American Academy of Anti-Aging and Regenerative Medicine is one of the fastest and largest growing body of trained health care professionals in this area, understanding the importance of this foundational pillar and how to work with these challenges.

Nutritional health is not just about eating clean which is certainly important. It is a knowledge base unto itself in recognizing what is imitation food, fillers, and unfortunate decliners of health which can lead to obesity, diabetes, hypertension, heart disease, cancer, reduced brain function and aberrant behaviors to name a few. The challenges faced by our physical body today are enormous and much greater than what our grandparents faced in a much less developed and technological age. We face an ever greater demand of components which our body requires everyday including vitamins, minerals, essential fatty acids, proteins or protein subcomponents and proper healthy carbohydrates. This is not guess work or pick and choose. With properly trained health professionals in this area, these individualized needs can be sorted out for what each person needs. Understanding the physical examination of the body and the signs that a trained professional can see with improper internal changes is paramount to getting what is needed. Specialty labs have raised the technology bar to provide the necessary answers to the questions that are needed. Health professionals with understanding and training in functional medicine can assist in these matters. Functional medicine, the nuts and bolts of giving the body what it needs, is designed for the individual and not mass health care of one size must fit everyone. The Institute of Functional Medicine in addition to the American Academy of Anti-Aging and Regenerative Medicine serves as another resource of trained individuals in this area.

Adequate regular exercise is what sets the above in motion. Being sedentary is a pause, so to speak, however, it is movement and strength resistance which infuses our systems with input that is needed. Whether it be through individual training on a treadmill, elliptical, stepper or group sessions with dance, yoga, boot camps or weight pump sessions, all can serve one well. Get started and pick one. Grow from there, mix it up and do YOUR thing.

With the foundational pillars in place for the physical well-being, other life enhancing measures can deliver remarkable personal advances. Recognizing the proper alignment of the psyche and mental energy now lifts one to even higher levels. Where does one start? Again, there are many sources touted as a means to reaching that destination. Speaking from my own personal journey, a few sources that I have found to be helpful extending well beyond my physical existence include the time sustaining teachings of Dr. Carl Jung and the collective unconsciousness. The detailed work by Dr. Brian Weiss touches on the therapeutic connection of the past with now through past life regression therapy. Carrying development and life purpose studies even further is the extensive body of work by Dr. Michael Newton in "Life Between Lives". It takes one to the spiritual plane of understanding, learning and teaching and its relevance to you.

Everyone has their own map of health and destiny. Open your eyes, wake up and realize the resources are there for you. Participate in the design and utilize what you need to make this life the best you deserve.

Chapter 13: Your Wealth

Calculating the amount of wealth you have is more easily measured than figuring out how much "health" you have. None-the-less the question of how much wealth is enough is more subjective. We can look at how much wealth is necessary to meet your needs and then look at wants. We took a very broad look this in Chapter 8. As with health books have been written on building or creating wealth. The real question for YOU is "how do I optimize ME"? How much wealth do you need and what is the best approach to get there. It should be noted that wealth can be defined in many ways and some would consider time one of their most precious assets. We don't disagree! For the discussion in this chapter we are only looking at monetary wealth.

First and foremost we need enough income to cover our basic needs – food, shelter, clothing, utilities, etc. Then we can look at our wants – hobbies, gifts, charitable giving, etc. Once we determine needs and wants we can then look at what sources of income we have now or will have in the future. The amount of wealth that is needed will depend on what your needs and wants are, how long you will need to fund these expenses, how much your expenses will increase over time and a myriad of other factors. If we invest with greater growth potential we may experience greater volatility but potentially reach our goal faster. If we can minimize income tax we may be able to have a lower overall return but have more money in our pocket. Evaluating how much money you need now and in the future is a critical area that your financial advisor can provide real assistance with. Determining an asset allocation that meets both your needs and also risk tolerance while being consistent with realistic expectations is another area that your advisor can assist you.

One important side note. While we often are told that all debt is bad — this is not always the case. If we can borrow money at a rate lower than we can earn on our investments we can 'make money with our money'. For example if we have a 5% mortgage and can invest in a fixed rate bond at 7% then it does not make sense to pay down or pay off that debt. There may be other reasons that having some debt makes sense. Having some "good debt" may actually help you to build wealth. This is another area that your financial advisor can assist you with.

There are many paths that can lead to "DW", Destination Wealth just as there are many paths leading to Destination Health. Ultimately that path(s) you choose will depend upon your needs, objectives, risk tolerance and time-frame. For some, one path will suffice. However, for many one path is not sufficient to reach that all-encompassing destination of optimal wealth. You will know when you are there because you will feel a sense of comfort where you are not concerned about day to day needs and can enjoy many of your wants. Once you are there, you will be open to living life experiences totally unencumbered by financial constraints.

Chapter 14: Happiness

Are successful people happy because they are successful or are they successful because they are happy? Science and personal experience suggests the latter. The idea that if we just make more or do more money, or achieve a new position at work will make us happy is misleading at best and at worst leads to disappointment and frustration. The idea that we control how happy we are — regardless of circumstances and ultimately control our own success may be hard to believe but is true. While we have discussed ways to be improve your health and wealth in this book ultimately we are discussing how to be happier.

The benchmarks for most things that scientists track are the averages. The measure of happiness while tougher to define is no exception. If we study what is merely average, we will remain merely average. If we want to be exceptional we need to study the exceptional. This is true with our health, happiness and financial well being. The good news is that success leaves clues.

Shawn Achor is the author of the best selling book The Happiness Advantage. He spent 12 years researching Happiness at Harvard University. Mr. Achor postulates that when we stop studying the average and begin researching positive outliers -- people who are above average for a positive dimension like optimism or intelligence -- a wildly different picture emerges. Our daily decisions and habits have a huge impact upon both our levels of happiness and success. More importantly we can utilize specific exercises to increase our level of happiness and thereby our success (however we define it).

So is it that many successful people are happy because they are successful or they are successful because they are happy? There are many people that society deems successful who are unhappy . Take students at Harvard who have the opportunity to attend one of the greatest learning institutions and who are generally very smart folks often feel that they are not successful if they are not in the top 1% of their class and therefore 99% of them will potentially be disappointed.

The first thing we must do is to change our behavior to see the positive. If I want something I've never had I must do something I've never done. The truth is ... change involves desire, decisions, and doing. A change of mind results in a change of heart, which results in a change of action, which results in a change of feelings. All of that can be a little scary ... doing something you've never done. So heed the advice of educator L. Thomas Holdcroft, "The past is a guidepost, not a hitching post." On the other hand things that I do not take action on are probably not going to change. You may whine and complain about your weight, your spouse, your kids, your job, your team, or letting your phone and e-mail ruin your life. But as much as I hate to say this, you have no right to complain about any of those things if you don't do something about them or if you just keep on permitting them to happen.

Worry is negative goal setting - thinking about everything that has or can go wrong. To worry about what you can't change is useless. To worry about you can change is a waste of time; either change it or forget it. Dale Carnegie, "If you can't sleep, then get up and do something instead of lying there and worrying. It's the worry that gets you, not the loss of sleep."

Even when we are awake a recent study showed that people spend 46.9 percent of their waking hours thinking about something other than what they're doing, and this mind-wandering typically makes them unhappy. So says a study that used an iPhone web app to gather 250,000 data points on subjects' thoughts, feelings, and actions as they went about their lives.

The research, by psychologists Matthew A. Killingsworth and Daniel T. Gilbert of Harvard University, stated "A human mind is a wandering mind, and a wandering mind is an unhappy mind," Killingsworth and Gilbert write. "The ability to think about what is not happening is a cognitive achievement that comes at an emotional cost."

Positive psychology is "the scientific study of optimal human functioning" and was first introduced as a field of study by Dr. Martin Seligman in 1998, when he was President of the American Psychological Association.

While psychology has traditionally concerned itself with what ails the human mind—such as anxiety, depression, neurosis, obsessions, paranoia, and delusions—Dr. Seligman and other pioneers in positive psychology asked the following question: "What are the enabling conditions that make human beings flourish?"

The good news is that positive psychology shows that you can learn to be happier just as you can learn a foreign language or to be proficient at a sport. This rapidly growing field is shedding light on what makes us happy, the pursuit of happiness, and how we can lead more fulfilling, satisfying lives.

We recommend reading the books below which will go into more detail on things you can do to improve your happiness. A few exercises to consider.

Ask yourself questions to foster awareness about what actions and attitudes will make you happier. For example keeping a Happiness Journal where each day we write down three things we are grateful for. This will help you look for things in your life that make you happy.

You may also consider sending a personal note each day to someone who has positively impacted your life.

Imagine yourself as 110 years old. What advice would you give your younger self? This added perspective will allow you to recognize and eliminate the trivial and negative things from your life

In his book "Happiness" Dr. Ben-Shahar suggest creating rituals or daily habits. "The most creative individuals — whether artists, businesspeople, or parents — have rituals that they follow. Paradoxically, the routine frees them up to be creative and spontaneous."

Simplify. Identify what's most important to you and focus on that; stop trying to do too much. People who take on too much experience time poverty, which inhibits their ability to derive happiness from any of the activities they participate in.

Keep in mind that happiness is mostly dependent on your state of mind. Barring extreme circumstances, our level of well being is determined by what we choose to focus on and by our interpretation of external events.

It is important to note that happiness is not an end state, but rather something you work towards your whole life. We definitely want to be content and appreciative of our current situation but should also continue to grow. Thus as content as you are, you can be happier each day. Happiness is a journey, not a destination where we balance having what we want with wanting what we have.

Books to read on the subject

> Dr. Ben-Shahar- Happiness

> Shawn Achor – The Happiness Advantage

Chapter 15: Master Trip Planner

"The journey of a thousand miles begins with a single step."
— Lao Tzu

The Master Trip Planner will help organize where you go from here for yourself and will also provide a nice tool to use with your medical and financial professionals. Achieving your vision may seem like a daunting task but you have already done much of the work in chapters 1, 2 and 5. The next step is writing down your goals and vision!

This planner will help you define your vision and turn your goals into a reality. You may use it as is or modify it to suit your needs. The important thing is to write out your goals, vision and timeline. Writing out your action plan will make your vision concrete. This will help you decide on strategies to meet your objectives and to set up a time frame for doing so. Whether you utilize our guide – or develop your own- writing down your goals and vision is a very powerful tool. Consider the following.

Why do 3% of Harvard MBAs Make Ten Times as Much as the Other 97% Combined ? The answer is that they have clearly written goals. In 1979, interviewers asked new graduates from the Harvard's MBA Program a simple question: "Have you set clear, written goals for your future and made plans to accomplish them?"

What they found was that:

> 84% had no specific goals at all

> 13% had goals but they were not committed to paper

> 3% had clear, written goals and plans to accomplish them

In 1989, the interviewers again interviewed the graduates of that class. You can guess the results:

> The 13% of the class who had goals were earning, on average, twice as much as the 84% who had no goals at all.

> Even more staggering – the 3% who had clear, written goals were earning, on average, ten times as much as the other 97% put together.

(Source: <u>What They Don't Teach You in the Harvard Business School</u>, *by Mark McCormack*)

So here we go!

Vision:

Write down the four items from chapter one that you listed as your *call to action*. These are the items and time frame that you listed as things you could do today to achieve your dream life in the future.

1. _____

2. _____

3. _____

4. _____

In Chapter 1 you listed the 3 top three things that impact your overall health today. Please list these.

1. _____

2. _____

3. _____

In Chapter 1 you listed your three most important financial goals – write them down here.

1. _____

2. _____

3. _____

Take some time and write down WHY the above goals are important to you and how your life will improve if you meet all of these.

_____

_____

_____

_____

List the top three things you need to do – in the following time periods – to move on the path of achieving the above vision. Take a look at your immediate plan in Chapter 5.

1. _____

2. _____

3. _____

In the next 30 days the top three things I will do are:

Financially:

1. _____

2. _____

3. _____

For my health

1. _____

2. _____

3. _____

For personal and professional happiness

1. _____

2. _____

3. _____

Compare the above to your action plan from Chapter 5. Rewrite out your action plan from Chapter 5.

Each 30 days is a good time to evaluate progress, look at success and plan for the next stage. The only failure is when you don't try. As long as you are trying there is only success and learning experiences so you can adjust your behavior in the next 30 days!

Write our your diet and exercise plan for the next 30 days. You don't have to do daily menus but think about what foods you will eat, how much and when. Carve our time for exercise and write out a program now.

_____

_____

_____

_____

Finally, write down the professionals you will contact in the next 30 – 90 days as appropriate.

Doctor(s): When do I contact? Who?

_____

Financial advisor: When do I contact? Who?

_____

Legal Advisor: Do I need at this time? If yes when and who?

_____

Insurance Review: Can my financial advisor do this? Do I need to have reviewed? Who?

_____

Tax and Accounting: Do I need? If yes when and who?

_____

If I do not have a specific person who can I speak to about a referral? List names here

_____

_____

_____

What questions do I have for my professional advisors?

_____

_____

_____

You will be happier, healthier and more financially secure in the next 30 days and for the rest of your life if you follow your own path. Very small changes today will make a huge impact over the rest of your life in terms of health, financial well being and happiness. You have now taken more steps on your journey to 'optimize yourself' – congratulations.

Chapter 16: Starting Thoughts

"Your habits become your values, Your values become your destiny." – Mahatma Gandhi

While this is the last chapter of the book we consider these starting thoughts as you are just beginning your journey to better health, wealth and happiness. Completing this book is the first step on a life long journey. You have taken some major steps on your road to better health, wealth and happiness. You knew you wanted to do something and took action by reading this book. You then took the time and had the discipline to read and consider the contents. Congratulations – you have done more than most people!

Now where you go is up to you! As with many things what you get out of this book will depend on what you put into the process. You may want to go back and revisit some of the worksheets and think about how the material relates to you and your personal goals. As mentioned in the first chapters the tools for improving your life are not difficult to utilize – but it is not easy because it takes consistency, discipline and vision.

We recommend working through the worksheets and also thinking about what you want and where you are. Once you have time to process, consider and revise the information you can then work with your professional advisors to move on to the next step. The following appendices will provide additional information for you to consider and should be viewed as a reference keeping in mind some of the topics may not apply to your specific situation.

One of the most important things you can do is to think about and visualize what you want. Desire without action will not achieve many things. For example wishing you will have enough savings or lose weight but doing nothing about it will not yield results. But with just a little practice anyone can enter a state of mind that improves human capability... a state of 'heightened awareness,' where anything is possible!

The autonomic nervous system controls your breathing, pulse, glands etc. You do not consciously have to think about breathing but you breathe. While there are all kinds of process running in your body you can consciously choose what you will think about and this can effect physiological changes.

Imagination can cause you to age faster... or age more slowly... it can cause an ulcer... or heal an ulcer. Medical case histories are filled with stories of people who have had miraculous recoveries or were literally scared to death. What would a coroner write on such a death report—"cause of death: imagination"?

Here is a quick example of the power of the human mind: First, suspend your natural disbelief, just for a minute, while you try this exercise. It's easy and everyone can, do it. It will only take a few seconds.

First relax and take a deep breath and clear your mind; now use your imagination and try to clearly picture this in as much detail as possible:

You have a bright yellow, ripe lemon in the palm of your hand. Rub the skin of the fruit with your hands. Feel the texture. Smell it. Now pick up a sharp knife and slice slowly through the lemon. Juice squirts and runs out of the lemon onto your hand. Put a drop of juice on your finger and touch it to your tongue. Is it terribly sour?

For most people, just a simple little exercise like this will cause their mouth to water.

Doctors will tell you that mouth-watering is an involuntary reflex of the autonomic nervous system. Or, to put that in layman's terms, you can't physically control it. However, you can use your imagination to think of lemons... and that will do the trick.

Does it make you wonder... what else can the imagination control? It is vastly more powerful than most people realize.

We've all had the experience of preparing for something important; maybe a big speech, maybe calling a potential employer, client, or even a first date, when simply "imagining" what would happen caused our hearts to race and our palms to sweat. But can the imagination control influences from outside the body? The answer is yes!

Once you gain control of what and how your visualize – positive or negative you can truly impact your life. The tools in this book focus on many practical aspects of improving your life but ultimately it is up to you to figure out what you want and then to think about it in a positive way. Success depends on both vision and action. Doing one without the other will rarely produce optimal results if any. Simply thinking about doing something and not doing won't accomplish anything. On the other hand taking action that is not consistent with our ultimate goal will not be productive and can be exhaustive. We need vision, action and then a review of what we are doing. We need to reassess what we are doing and modify it. Rarely will we get it right the first time. Those who have acheived exceptional success have often done so based upon what they have learned from actions that have not worked rather than those that have. Be persistent, be bold, be open to change and you will succeed.

You are encouraged to contact the authors with your stories of success, questions and thoughts. Congratulations and bon voyage!

About the Authors

Jack Anstandig, M.D. has served as a Neurologist for 25 years and has also dedicated himself to leveraging the holistic approach to health by incorporating mind, body and spirit principals into his patient care. Dr Anstandig is currently the medical director for BodyLogic MD of Las Vegas where he devotes his wellness based practice in helping women and men overcoming health challenges which may not sufficiently addressed by traditional medicine.

Dr Anstandig obtained his Bachelor of Science degree and Doctorate from the University of Pittsburgh. His internship training in Internal Medicine was completed at the Western Pennsylvania Hospital in Pittsburgh, Pennsylvania. Specialty training in Neurology was achieved at the Cleveland Clinic Foundation in Cleveland, Ohio. He also served as Chief Resident in Neurology, integrating education and training for the Cleveland Clinic program. Following his training, he served in the United States Air Force as a Major treating active duty personnel, their dependents and veterans. He was awarded the United States Air Force Commendation Medal for Meritorious Service. Advancing in his career, he opened a clinical based practice in Neurology in Cleveland, Ohio. During these years he continued to pursue further education and training in the holistic health field including acupuncture, fellowship training in anti-aging and regenerative medicine, natural therapies , clinical hypnotherapy, past life regression therapy and vibrational healing.

Concurrent to his direct patient care activities, Dr. Anstandig also served as an educator and national lecturer for physicians, nurses, healthcare personal and community groups teaching about various medical conditions and treatment options to optimize heath.

Through the years of professional practice involving thousands of patient contacts, Dr Anstandig's paramount focus and dedication has been his unwavering compassion and care in working with and uniquely treating each individual that has been in contact with him. He currently resides, practices and continues to explore and expand new healing therapies in Las Vegas, Nevada.

Dr. Anstandig now lives and practices in Las Vegas, Nevada and can be reached via via email at **drjack@optimizemebook.com**

Randy Carver, is President of Carver Financial Services Inc. an independent registered investment advisor and a registered principal with Raymond James Financial Services Inc. (member FINRA/SIPC). As of 2013 Carver Financial Services manages in excess of $850 million for clients globally.

Randy has worked in the financial services industry since 1986 and founded Carver Financial Services Inc. in 1990. Randy holds a degree in economics from Oberlin College and post graduate degrees in finance. Randy is a General Securities Principal (Series 24 license), Municipal Securities Representative (Series 53 license) Commodities Principal (series 31), holds Series 7 and Series 63 securities licenses, in addition to life, health and variable annuity insurance licenses. Randy has earned the Chartered Retirement Planning Counselor® designation from The College for Financial Planning®.

The October 2013 issue of Barron's named Randy Carver as one of the Top 1,000 advisors in the United States . The rankings are based on data provided by the nation's most productive advisors. Randy and his team have been recognized by Barrons' magazine and also Registered Rep Magazine every year since 2008. Registered Rep's America's Top 100 Independent Broker/Dealer Advisors award based upon assets under management, and other subjective factors not disclosed by the magazine, for advisors with $150 million in assets or greater.

Randy has taught Accountancy Board approved CPE courses and Supreme Court Commission on Continuing Legal Education approved courses for attorneys since 1987. One of the most sought after economic experts in the United States Randy was featured as one of the "50 Most Interesting People in Cleveland" by *Cleveland Magazine* and has appeared as an expert commentator on *FOX*, *CNN* and *CNNfn TV, USA Today, the New York Times and The Wall Street Journal.*

Randy lives in Kirtland Hills, Ohio and may be contacted by email at: drrandycarver@gmail.com or via phone at (440) 974-0808

On the web at **www.carverfinancialservices.com**

Appendix I: Key Estate Planning Documents & Checklist

There are six estate planning documents you will want to consider regardless of your age or net worth:

1. Durable power of attorney

2. Medical power of attorney

3. Advanced medical directives

4. Will

5. Letter of instruction

6. Living trust

This is a very basic list. The following is meant to serve as a guide in speaking with your attorney, not a replacement for doing so. There are other types of legal documents that you may want to consider depending upon your situation. Your estate planning advisor can assist with this.

Durable power of attorney

A durable power of attorney (DPOA) can help protect your property in the event you become unwilling or unable to handle financial or other personal matters.. If no one is ready to look after your financial affairs when you can't, your property may be wasted, abused, or lost. A DPOA allows you to authorize someone else to act on your behalf, so he or she can do things like register a car, pay expenses, collect benefits, watch over your investments, and file taxes.

There are two types of DPOAs: (1) a standby DPOA, which is effective immediately (this is appropriate if you face a serious operation or illness), and (2) a springing DPOA, which is not effective unless you have become incapacitated. Please note that a springing DPOA is not permitted in some states, so you'll want to check with an attorney.

Medical power of attorney

A medical power of attorney (MPOA) is similar to a durable power of attorney but specifically for medical care. You can name a different person as your medical power of attorney than someone who has a general durable power to handle your general affairs. When you draft your medical power of attorney -- sometimes this is also referred to as a "durable power of attorney for health care" -- you name a trusted person to oversee your medical care and make health care decisions for you if you are unable to do so. Depending on where you live, the person you appoint may be called your "agent," "attorney-in-fact," "health care proxy," "health care surrogate," or something similar.

Your health care agent will work with doctors and other health care professionals to make sure you get the kind of medical care you wish to receive. When arranging your care, your agent is legally bound to follow your treatment preferences to the extent that he or she knows about them.

To make your wishes clear, you can use a second type of health care directive -- often called a "health care declaration" or "living will" -- to provide written health care instructions to your agent and health care providers. To make this easier, some states combine a durable power of attorney for health care and health care declaration into a single form, commonly called an "advance health care directive." (see below). It is often possible to obtain a free form medical POA reviewed for legality in your state, from a local hospital. You will still want to have your legal advisor review the form to make sure it reflects your wishes.

Advanced medical directives

Advanced medical directives- sometimes called a living will- let others know what medical treatment you would want, or allows someone to make medical decisions for you, in the event you can't express your wishes yourself. If you don't have an advanced medical directive on file , medical care providers must prolong your life using artificial means, if necessary. With today's technology, physicians can sustain you for days and weeks (if not months or even years).

There are three types of advanced medical directives. Each state allows only a certain type (or types). You may find that one, two, or all three types are necessary to carry out all of your wishes for medical treatment. (Just make sure all documents are consistent.)

First, a living will allows you to approve or decline certain types of medical care, even if you will die as a result of that choice. In most states, living wills take effect only under certain circumstances, such as terminal injury or illness. Generally, one can be used only to decline medical treatment that "serves only to postpone the moment of death." In those states that do not allow living wills, you may still want to have one to serve as evidence of your wishes.

Second, a durable power of attorney for health care (known as a health-care proxy in some states) allows you to appoint a representative to make medical decisions for you. You decide how much power your representative will or won't have.

Finally, a Do Not Resuscitate order (DNR) is a doctor's order that tells medical personnel not to perform CPR if you go into cardiac arrest. There are two types of DNRs. One is effective only while you are hospitalized. The other is used while you are outside the hospital.

Will

A will is often said to be the cornerstone of any estate plan. The main purpose of a will is to disburse property to heirs after your death. If you don't leave a will, disbursements will be made according to state law, which might not be what you would want.

There are two other equally important aspects of a will:

1. You can name the person (executor) who will manage and settle your estate. If you do not name someone, the court will appoint an administrator, who might not be someone you would choose.

2. You can name a legal guardian for minor children or dependents with special needs. If you don't appoint a guardian, the state will appoint one for you.

Keep in mind that a will is a legal document, and the courts are very reluctant to overturn any provisions within it. Therefore, it's crucial that your will be well written and articulated, and properly executed under your state's laws.

Letter of instruction

A letter of instruction (also called a testamentary letter or side letter) is an informal, nonlegal document that generally accompanies your will and is used to express your personal thoughts and directions regarding what is in the will (or about other things, such as your burial wishes or where to locate other documents). This can be the most helpful document you leave for your family members and your executor.

Unlike your will, a letter of instruction remains private. Therefore, it is an opportunity to say the things you would rather not make public.

A letter of instruction is not a substitute for a will. Any directions you include in the letter are only suggestions and are not binding. The people to whom you address the letter may follow or disregard any instructions.

Living trust

A living trust (also known as a revocable or inter vivos trust) is a separate legal entity you create to own property, such as your home or investments. The trust is called a living trust because it's meant to function while you're alive. You control the property in the trust, and, whenever you wish, you can change the trust terms, transfer property in and out of the trust, or end the trust altogether.

Not everyone needs a living trust, but it can be used to accomplish various purposes. The primary function is typically to avoid probate. This is possible because property in a living trust is not included in the probate estate.

Depending on your situation and your state's laws, the probate process can be simple, easy, and inexpensive, or it can be relatively complex, resulting in delay and expense. This may be the case, for instance, if you own property in more than one state or in a foreign country, or have heirs that live overseas.

Further, probate takes time, and your property generally won't be distributed until the process is completed. A small family allowance is sometimes paid, but it may be insufficient to provide for a family's ongoing needs. Transferring property through a living trust provides for a quicker, almost immediate transfer of property to those who need it. *Living trusts do not generally minimize federal estate taxes or protect property from future creditors.*

Probate can also interfere with the management of property like a closely held business or stock portfolio. *Although your executor is responsible for managing the property until probate is completed, he or she may not have the expertise or authority to make significant management decisions, and the property may lose value. Transferring the property with a living trust can result in a smoother transition in management.*

Finally, avoiding probate may be desirable if you're concerned about privacy. Probated documents (e.g., will, inventory) become a matter of public record. Generally, a trust document does not. Although a living trust transfers property like a will, you should still also have a will because the trust will be unable to accomplish certain things that only a will can, such as naming an executor or a guardian for minor children. In addition the will can direct any assets not already titled in the name of the trust to 'pour over' into the trust.

Guardianship Papers

A consideration for those who have young or special needs children is who would be responsible for their care in the event of your death or incapacity. It should be noted that you can name one person as guardian of the child and another person (or institution) as guardian of their estate. For example a trusted friend or family member could be the legal guardian for your children and a trust company could handle their investments.

As time passes your needs and vision may change along with the estate planning law. It is important to periodically review and update all of your estate planning documents. For the average person this should be every three to four years. For a more complex situation it could be as often as annually.

Estate Planning Checklist- discussion with attorney

General information	Yes	No	N/A
1. Has relevant personal information been gathered? • Personal details • Family details • Current advisory team • Goals and expectations			
2. Has financial situation been assessed? • Assets • Liabilities • Life insurance policies • Other insurance coverage • Income • Expenses			
3. Have current documents been reviewed? • Will • Trust documents • Power of attorneys • Medical directives • Insurance policies • Buy-sell agreements • Deeds, leases, mortgages, and land contracts • Guardian nominations • Separation/divorce agreements • Tax returns			
4. Have funeral arrangements been made?			
Notes:			

Basics	Yes	No	N/A
1. Is there currently a valid will?			
2. If yes, does will reflect current goals and objectives?			
3. Does choice of executor remain appropriate?			
4. Has durable power of attorney been executed?			
5. Have medical directives been executed?			
6. Have beneficiary designations for retirement plans and life insurance policies been reviewed?			
7. Has impact of probate been considered?			

Notes:

Trusts	Yes	No	N/A
1. Is the use of a living trust appropriate?			
2. Is the use of a testamentary trust appropriate?			
3. Is the use of an irrevocable life insurance trust appropriate?			
4. Do existing trusts, if any, continue to meet overall objectives?			

Notes:

Estate tax	Yes	No	N/A
1. Has estate plan been reviewed due to changing tax laws?			
2. Has impact of estate tax been evaluated?			
3. Have options to minimize estate tax been explored? • Lifetime gifting • Full use of basic (applicable) exclusion amount and marital deduction • Qualified terminable interest property (QTIP) elections • Qualified domestic trust (QDT) for noncitizen spouse • Charitable giving • Grantor retained trusts • Family limited partnership (FLP)/limited liability company (LLC)			

Notes:

Lifetime gifting	Yes	No	N/A
1. Have gifts been made?			
2. Has a lifetime gifting strategy been implemented?			
3. Are gift tax consequences understood?			
4. Has consideration been given to types of property suitable for gifting?			
5. Is valuation discount planning understood?			

Notes:

Charitable intentions	Yes	No	N/A
1. Have charitable gifts or bequests been planned?			
2. Is a charitable trust appropriate? • Charitable lead trust • Charitable remainder trust • Pooled income fund • Private foundation • Donor-advised fund			
3. Is a charitable gift annuity appropriate?			
4. Is the charitable gift of a remainder interest in a home or farm appropriate?			

Notes:

Life insurance issues	Yes	No	N/A
1. Have liquidity needs of estate at death been evaluated?			
2. Is current life insurance coverage appropriate?			
3. Have steps been taken to keep life insurance proceeds out of taxable estate? • Policy ownership • Irrevocable life insurance trust			
4. Have beneficiary choices been evaluated in light of overall estate plan?			
Notes:			

Business interests	Yes	No	N/A
1. Have provisions been made to transfer business interest? • Buy-sell agreement and necessary funding • Sell business • Transfer business with lifetime gifts • Key person buyout			
2. Is liquidation an option?			

Notes:

Appendix 2:
Will You Outlive Your Money?

The best time to figure out how much money you'll need in retirement is well before you are retired. One of the biggest concerns for retirees is whether they will outlive their retirement savings and run out of money. Whether you might run out of money or not depends on a number of factors including, but not limited to: how much money you have, how long you need the funds to last, how much income you need to draw currently, and what your tax situation looks like. Just to name a few. You'll be better off if you can tackle these issues before you retire but if you are retired and have concerns about your funds being depleted there are several steps you can take even at this late date. The following are tips and ideas to help make sure you don't outlive your money.

Tips to help make your savings last longer

While it may seem obvious one of the best ways to extend retirement savings is by adjusting your spending habits. You might be able to get by with only minor changes to your spending habits, but if your savings are far below your projected needs and desires more drastic changes may be necessary. Spending less and saving even a little money can really add up if you do it consistently and earn a reasonable rate of return.

Make major changes to your spending patterns

The following are some suggested changes you may choose to implement:

Consolidate any outstanding loans to reduce your interest rate or monthly payment. Consider using home equity financing for this purpose.

If your home mortgage is paid in full, weigh the pros and cons of a reverse mortgage to increase your cash flow.

Reduce your housing expenses by moving to a less expensive home or apartment.

If you are still paying off your home mortgage, consider refinancing your mortgage if interest rates have dropped since you took the loan.

Sell your second car, especially if it is only used occasionally.

Shop around for less expensive insurance and decide if you even need certain types of insurance. For example if you don't have a lot of debt and no dependents why pay for expensive life insurance? Often you can save a lot a year (and even more over a period of years) by switching to insurance policies that have lower premiums, but that still provide the coverage you need. Life, auto and health insurance are the three types of insurance where you probably stand to save the most, since premiums can go up dramatically with age and declining health. Consult your insurance professional.

Have your child enroll in or transfer to a less expensive college (a state university as opposed to a private one, for example). This can be a particularly good idea if the cheaper college has a strong reputation and can provide a quality education.

Make minor changes to your spending patterns. You would be surprised how quickly your savings add up when you implement a written budget and make several small changes to your spending patterns. If you have only minor concerns about making your retirement last (or even grow) , small changes to your spending habits may be enough to correct this problem. The following are several ideas you might consider when adjusting your spending patterns:

Switch to a lower interest credit card. Transfer your balances from higher interest cards and then cancel the old accounts.

Eat dinner at home, and carry "brown-bag" lunches instead of eating out.

Consider buying a well-maintained used car instead of a new car.

Subscribe to the magazines and newspapers you read instead of paying full price at the newsstand.

Where possible, cut down on utility costs and other household expenses.

Plan your expenditures and avoid impulse buying.

Use caution when spending down your investment principal

Don't assume you'll be able to live on just the earnings from your investment portfolio and your retirement and investment accounts for the rest of your life. At some point, you will probably have to start drawing on the principal. You'll want to be careful not to spend too much too soon. This can be a great temptation particularly early in your retirement because the tendency is to travel extensively and buy the things you couldn't afford during your working years. A good guideline is to make sure you don't spend more than 4 percent of your principal during the first five years of retirement. If you whittle away your principal too quickly, you won't be able to earn enough on the remaining principal to carry you through the later years. The other temptation is to spend more in years where the portfolio does particularly well. It is important to keep withdrawals consistent as the extra growth in the good years provides a cushion for years when the portfolio has a lower or negative rate of return.

Portfolio review

It is important to make sure that your level of risk, your choice of investment vehicles, and your asset allocation are appropriate based upon your changing needs, tax laws and considering your long-term objectives. While you don't want to lose your investment principal, you also don't want to lose out to inflation. A regular review (we suggest at least every 6 months) of your investment portfolio is essential in determining if changes should be made and how long your money may last.

Continue to invest for growth

Traditional wisdom holds that retirees should value the safety of their principal above all else. For this reason, some people totally shift their investment portfolio to fixed-income investments, such as bonds and money market accounts, as they approach retirement. As outlined in Chapter 10 the problem with this approach is that it completely ignores the effects of inflation. You will actually lose money if the return on your investments does not keep up with inflation. The allocation of your portfolio should generally become progressively more conservative as you grow older, but it is wise to consider maintaining at least a portion of your portfolio in growth investments.

Basic rules of investment still apply during retirement

Although you will undoubtedly make changes to your investment portfolio as you reach retirement age, you should still bear in mind the basic rules of investing. Diversification and asset allocation remain important as you make the transition from accumulation to utilization.

Appendix 3: Budget & Income

A personal income statement will give you an idea of where you stand in terms of income and expense. Establishing a budget will help you track, plan, and control the inflow and outflow of income. By looking at what your income and expenses are you can determine where you stand and develop a plan against which you'll measure your progress.

The budgeting process begins with gathering the data that makes up your financial history It is important to be as accurate as possible – sometimes we have a tendency to under estimate some expenses or over estimate future income! Using the worksheet below we can use this information to do a cash flow analysis. This will allow you to periodically check your progress against the plan and make adjustments as needed. We recommend tracking actual expenses over 6 – 12 months and comparing it to your estimates. One way to do this is to pay all bills and expense from a single account.

You might have one or more major savings needs goals in mind, but now is the time to look at all your anticipated financial needs, including your cash reserve, and determine your goals. Knowing what all of your goals are enables you to create the best plan to achieve those objectives over the long term. While you may not be able to achieve all of your goals simultaneously, having a plan in place will help as you work toward your future goals.

Once you know where you stand financially and the goals you hope to achieve, you are in a position to design a plan that will move you expeditiously in that direction. You will know how aggressive you need to be in order to achieve the objectives you set, and therefore you can design a plan that fits both your resources and objectives.

Flexibility is always an important part of the planning process. As life's circumstances change, as they inevitably will, you will need to adjust your spending plan accordingly. The important point is that this process keeps you abreast of how these changes are occurring and allows you to make changes as you find them appropriate to your needs and resources. By having an accurate idea of what your current and anticipated expenses are you can start to figure out how much future income you will need. This allows you to develop a savings and investment plan using your own figures – not some 'rule of thumb' or average.

Remember that everyone's circumstances are unique. Consequently, what is reasonable for someone else might not be reasonable in your own situation? Frequently, there are underlying factors that influence what is reasonable for each individual. For example, someone with a chronic medical condition might reasonably es-timate much higher health-care expenses than someone who is consistently healthy.

The following worksheet is meant as a guide for you to develop your own. This will provide an idea of things to consider. There are also numerous online resources that you may utilize. The key is to pick something and then stick with it consistently to start develop-ing a picture of where you stand!

Monthly Budging Worksheet	
INCOME	
Salary # 1	
Salary # 2	
Bonus	
Social Security	
Pension	
Alimony (note how long this may continue)	
Inheritance (note if this is a one- time instance)	
Other income	
Total Income	
EXPENSES	
Housing	
Mortgage or rent	
Real Estate Tax	
Homeowners/renters Insurance	
Homeowners Association fees	
Estimated Annual Maintenance	
Larger Expense (replace roof, re-paint house, etc.)	
Lawn care/Snow Removal, etc.	
Utilities	
Electric	
Gas	
Water	

Cable TV / Internet	
Telephone (house and/or cell)	
Trash Removal	
Other	
Transportation	
Car Payment(s)	
Car Insurance	
Car Maintenance	
Gas	
Parking/Tolls	
License Plates/Registration	
Other	
Food & Entertainment	
Groceries	
Eating Out	
Entertainment (movies, concerts, etc.)	
Hobbies	
Recreational Vehicles (boat, PWC, RV, Snowmobile, etc.)	
Other	
Personal Care	
Dry cleaning/laundry	
New Clothing	
Hair/Nails/Massage	

Gym membership/Training	
Other	
Children	
Child care	
Clothing	
Tuition	
School Supplies	
Allowances	
Toys/Games/Entertainment	
Other	
Larger Expense/Savings	
Home improvement	
Appliance	
Vacation/Travel	
Charity/Church/Temple	
Other	
Other	
Healthcare (out of pocket)	
Doctors	
Dentist	
Therapist	
Eye Glasses/Contacts/Ophthalmologist	
Prescriptions	
Over The Counter Pharmacy	

Lab Work / Tests	
Hospital / Emergency	
Other Debt Service	
Student Loans	
Credit Card(s)	
Accounting/Legal Fee's	
Alimony Child Support	
Income Tax – Other Tax	
Total Expenses:	

Appendix 4:
Emergency Savings – Reserve

Inevitably life will throw us unexpected curves. The key is to be prepared for the unexpected. From a financial standpoint we recommend keeping an emergency reserve of cash or very short term fixed income holdings. Investments may include money market, bank and credit union accounts; short term certificates of deposit and possibly very short duration bonds or funds.

Everyone's situation is unique but as a general rule we recommend having 6 months living expenses in these types of investments as an emergency reserve. Keep in mind that the primary investment objective for your emergency cash reserve liquidity and safety, not return.

Having an emergency reserve will allow you to weather any unexpected storms including home repairs, unemployment, and medical bills. This will help protect other investments and avoid any penalties or income tax that might result from an unexpected withdrawal. At the very least, the emergency cash reserve should be sufficient to cover up to six months of the following:

> Mortgage payment

> Insurance costs

> Utility bills

> Groceries

> Fixed payments (car payments, student loan payments, tuition, etc.)

> Minimum payment on credit cards

> Routine professional fees such as doctors

> Prescriptions and basic home and car maintenance

We recommend building your emergency reserve before starting any other personal investment programs. One exception is if your employer offers a match on retirement plan contributions (such as 401(k), 403(b), etc.) in which case you should take care of contributing to your retirement plan at least to the fullest extent that will be matched.

Once you have your emergency reserve established you can then work on the other parts of your savings plan.

Appendix 5:
Long Term Care Insurance

Long Term Care insurance, also known as Nursing Home Insurance may be a key part of your asset protection strategy. With policies that have a home care rider this type of insurance may help you stay in your home and keep you out of a nursing home.

We insure our homes and cars but this is a way to insure our lifestyle. Consider some of these startling statistics:

> For a couple turning 65, there is a 70% chance that one of them will need long-term care. – Wall Street Journal

> As the Baby Boomers age, the number keeps rising. Now experts say that 65% of people over 75 need long term care. The average facility stay for older folks is about 3 years. (This is nursing home only stay estimate and does not include home care or assisted living, which usually come first.) – Business Week

> 97% of people over age 85 require assistance in the last year of life. – The LTC Report

> Singles are at risk, because they're usually not with someone who can properly care for them. The same is true for wives who tend to outlast their husbands by seven year average. – JB Quinn

> Over 50% of all people entering a care situation are penniless within one year. – Harvard University

> By 2018, a private room will cost over $500/day ($188,000/year). – LTCIP Academy

There are two main types of long term care insurance – health long term care and life long term care. Each of these may provide for home care or assisted living expenses. The life long term care policy utilizes an annuity or life insurance policy which allows access to the death benefit for long term care expenses. . Beginning in 2010, LTCI benefits paid from a combination policy are tax-free, if certain conditions are met. Also, cash value may be withdrawn from annuities or life insurance policies tax free to pay for qualified long term care expenses. You will want to check with your CPA and/or financial advisor as to the tax status of any withdrawals for your specific policy.

Traditional health long term care insurance is like car insurance – you pay an annual premium for your benefits. The premium may or may not be fixed.

When looking at long term care policies there are a number of considerations. First and foremost are what benefits are you seeking and what are the triggering events to collect your benefits.

Unfortunately, long term care (LTC) policies are not standardized--provisions contained in policies vary greatly, and premiums charged vary as well.

If you already own an LTC policy, you might wish to consider changing plans or upgrading coverage. You do not want to drop your current coverage until approved for the new policy. This would be appropriate if you're in good health and have an old LTC policy that was highly restrictive--perhaps it required you to have a prior hospital stay before benefits would begin. Most of the newer policies are less restrictive. Also, most of the newer policies offer inflation protection, another advantage.

How should you compare companies?

First it's important to review the financial strength of the companies you're interested in. You may do this by reviewing the company's A. M. Best Company's rating along with the opinions of other rating services, such as Moody's or Standard & Poor's Insurance Rating Services.

If you decide to go with an A. M. Best rating, you should select an insurance company that has received a rating of at least A or A+ from A. M. Best. This means that A.M Best feels the company is excellent or superior and entails very little risk.

Next, you need to read the actual policies carefully, making sure you understand each provision. After you've made sure that each policy contains the provisions you desire, you'll want to compare prices. Finally, you might want to consult with an agent, financial planner, or other professional to ensure that you've selected the policy that will best suit your needs. A professional advisor can also help with a cost benefit analysis of individual policies and decipher the differences between different alternatives.

The following is a partial list of items to consider when reviewing or comparing long term care insurance policies.

Features and benefits to compare	Explanation
Financial rating of insurance company	Is the insurance company financially stable? To determine this, review ratings published by A. M. Best, Standard & Poor's, Fitch, and others. If you have questions about the ratings, ask your insurance professional for assistance.
Tax-qualified or non-qualified policy	Is part of your premium payment tax deductible? Most policies are eligible for favorable tax treatment, which can lower your cost.
Availability of multiple facilities for care	Does the policy cover nursing homes, assisted-living facilities, and home health care? Many policies will cover care in all three settings.
Benefit period	How long will benefits be paid? Common options are 2, 3, 4, 5, 6, 8, 10 years, or lifetime benefits. The longer the benefit period, the more you will pay.
Benefit amount	How much will the policy pay per day if you need care? The most common maximum benefit amounts are $50 to $350 per day.
Benefit method	How are benefits paid? If the reimbursement method is used, only actual expenses are covered and the provider is reimbursed directly. If the indemnity method is used, the daily benefit amount specified in the contract is paid directly to the insured.
Pooled benefit	If the policy uses the reimbursement method of claims payment, does it include a pooled benefit feature? Under the reimbursement method, only your actual expenses are covered. If your actual expenses are less than your coverage amount, the pooled benefit feature allows you to save unused daily benefits for later. Without it, you forfeit any unused benefits.
Elimination (waiting) period	How long will you have to wait before benefits begin once you become medically eligible? Common options are 0, 30, 60, 90, 100, 180, or 365 days. The shorter the elimination period, the more you will pay.

Features and benefits to compare	Explanation
Recurrent claims	What happens if you recover but then need care again? Some policies require only one waiting period during the life of the policy, while others require a new waiting period when no benefit has been received for a period of time, usually 180 days.
Waiver of premium	Will you need to keep paying your LTCI premiums once you're receiving care? A waiver of premium option provides that no premium payments will be due while you are receiving benefits.
Activities of daily living (ADLs) requirement	What will trigger your eligibility for benefits? Find out how many ADLs (e.g., eating, bathing, and dressing) you must be unable to perform without assistance before a claim can be made. The fewer required the better. Available options range from two or three ADLs out of five or six.
Gatekeepers	What conditions must be satisfied in order to qualify for benefits? For example, you may need to be hospitalized for three days, receive paid professional services during the elimination period, and use caregivers who have certain credentials.
Inflation options	Will your benefit keep pace with the cost of living? A variety of options are available. No inflation protection means that your benefit amount will not increase, regardless of the increases in the cost of care. If you do not purchase inflation protection, you may be offered the opportunity to purchase increased benefits for an additional premium based on the increase in the cost of living at periodic intervals, such as every year or every three years. Other typical options include 5% simple or 5% compounded annual increases in benefit amounts. These options may allow for unlimited increases or an increase capped at two or three times the original benefit.
Reduced paid-up option	Does the policy include a reduced paid-up option? If so, the policy will pay some benefits even if you decide to stop paying the premiums.

Features and benefits to compare	Explanation
Return of premium at death option	Does the policy include a return of premium at death option? This refunds premiums if you die prematurely, but it generally applies only for deaths that occur before age 70.
Bed reservation benefit	Does the policy include a bed reservation benefit? This option will hold your place at the nursing home if you a have a hospital stay.
Other benefits	Does the policy offer any nonstandard benefits? These include respite care and care advisory services.
Exclusions to the contract	What coverage exclusions apply? Examples include pre-existing conditions excluded for a period of time after your policy is issued, and mental or emotional disorders without an organic disease.
Premium per $10/day of benefit	What premium will you pay? The biggest factor in determining premiums is age, but the options you choose count, too. Compare the cost of each option for each policy, and not just the total premium that includes all of the options you want.
Spousal discounts	Will you receive a discount if both you and your spouse buy a policy? Discounts of 10% to 20% are sometimes available to one or both spouses if both buy a policy.

Appendix 6: Diet and Exercise

The focus of this book is to Optimize You. Your diet and level of exercise will be an integral part of this process. As such we would be remiss if we didn't include something on these topics. The following is a very general overview and not a substitute for working with your healthcare team or doing further research on your own.

There are thousands of books, videos and programs offering instant results. Millions of dollars are spent each year on fad diets, exercise programs and equipment that ends up being a cloths rack rather than used for exercise. The truth is that there is no instant solution. The good news is that you can easily make huge improvements in your diet and level of fitness with a common sense approach and not going to extremes. As with many things discussed in this book the answer is simple – but not easy. It takes a little time, persistence and patience but you will be rewarded.

We offer the following suggestions as a general guide. You personal needs will be based on your current fitness level, diet and health as well as your personal goals. We recommend working with both your healthcare team (doctor, nutritionist etc.) and perhaps a certified personal trainer to develop a plan that works for you.

Drink enough water- 6 to 8 glasses per day

Get 30 minutes of physical activity in six days a week- this could be as simple as taking a walk.

Eat a number of small meals spaced out during the day. Most experts recommend breakfast, then a healthy snack mid morning, lunch, a snack, dinner and then another healthy snack. If you eat more it may help your body boost it's metabolism whereas if your body thinks it's starving your metabolism will actually slow down and you could burn less calories

Be aware of what you are eating and aim for a diet composed of a balance between fat, protein and carbohydrates.

Eat enough to meet your needs. The number of calories you need to consume will depend upon your activity level, body type and metabolism. Someone running ultra marathons may need 10,000 or more calories to sustain themselves where as a sedentary person only burns 1,000. It's not just the number of calories that's important it is the type. 1,000 fat calories is different than 1,000 protein. Diesel fuel and gasoline may have the same number of BTU's but you can't put diesel in your car without problems!

According to the 2010 Dietary Guidelines for Americans, healthful diets contain the amounts of essential nutrients and energy needed to prevent nutritional deficiencies and excesses. Healthful diets also provide the right balance of carbohydrates, fat, and protein to reduce risks for chronic diseases, and they are obtained from a variety of foods that are available, affordable, and enjoyable.

Consider doing some resistance weight training – after being properly taught and advised – three times per week

As with most things any program that sounds too good to be true – probably is! This goes for get rich quick schemes, exercise equipment and fad diets. The results you see will happen over time if you stick with your program. There is no need for expensive equipment or complicated diets – eating properly and getting a little exercise will yield significant results. Building wealth, better fitness and health take time Change may seem small but will compound over time – just like the penny!

Index

A

Account executives, 74
Achor, Shawn, 86
Action plans, 38–43
Activities of daily living (ADL) requirements, 137
Advanced medical directives, 107–108
Advanced practice registered nurses (APRNs), 77
Advisors, 72–79. *See also* Financial advisors; Medical advisors
Age management strategies, 33–36
Age Wave, 31
Aging, effects of, 36, 80
A.M. Best Company insurance ratings, 135
American Academy of Anti-Aging and Regenerative Medicine, 81, 82
American Board of Anti-Aging and Regenerative Medicine, 79
American College of Bryn Mawr, 75
American Holistic Medical Association, 78
Anti-aging specialists, 79
Any occupation disability, 54
Applicability of goals, 38
APRNs (advanced practice registered nurses), 77
Assets
    allocation of, 45–46
    financial, 23
    hard, 46
    non-personal, 52
    personal, 51–52
    protection of, 23, 51–55
Attorney-in-fact, 106
Autonomic nervous system, 99, 100

B

Baby boomers, 31, 133
Bed reservation benefits, 138
Behavioral finance, 60

Behaviors, consistency with values, 6–7, 38
Benchmarks for goals, 56–59
Bengen, William P., 57
Ben-Shahar, Tal, 89
Biases in decision-making, 60
Blood pressure levels, 24
Body mass index, 24
Bones, effects of aging on, 36
Broker-dealer firms, 74
Budgeting process, 125–130

C
Cardiovascular system, effects of aging on, 36
Career goals, 12–13
Carnegie, Dale, 87
Cash flow analysis, 125
Cash investments, 45, 46
Catastrophic medical expenses, 66
Certified Financial Planners® (CFPs), 74
Certified life underwriters (CLUs), 74, 75
Chartered financial consultants (ChFCs), 74, 75
Chiropractors, 78
Cholesterol levels, 24
Cognition and memory, effects of aging on, 36
Cognitive biases, 60
Collective unconsciousness, 83
Colonoscopies, 24
Commission-based financial advisors, 76
Compensation structures for financial advisors, 75–76
Compound benefits, 44–45
Consolidation of loans, 121
Conventional medical care, 80
Corporate stock, 69
Cost benefit analysis, 135
Cost of living, 23
Credit cards, tips for using, 122

D
Dalbar Inc., 67
Debt, 23, 85
Decision-making process, 60–63

Deferred compensation, 23
Diet and exercise, 82, 139–141
Dietary Guidelines for Americans (2010), 140
Dietitians, 79
Digestive system, effects of aging on, 36
Disability insurance, 53–55, 66
Doctors. *See* Physicians
Do not resuscitate (DNR) orders, 108
Durable power of attorney (DPOA), 105–106
Durable power of attorney for health care, 106–107, 108

E
Einstein, Albert, 44
Elimination periods, 136
Emergency reserve savings, 131–132
Endocrine system, effects of aging on, 36
Equity investments, 45, 46
Estate planning, 105–119
    advanced medical directives, 107–108
    checklist for, 112–119
    durable power of attorney, 105–106
    guardianship papers, 111
    letters of instruction, 109
    living trusts, 109–111
    medical power of attorney, 106–107
    objectives of, 23–24
    wills, 108–109
Excessive withdrawals, 66
Executor of will, 108
Exercise and diet, 82, 139–141
Expense sheets, 23

F
Family medicine, 77–78
Fasting blood sugar levels, 24
Fear, impact on financial goals, 66–67
Fee-based financial advisors, 76
Financial advisors
    compensation structures for, 75–76
    finding and selecting, 49–50
    role of, 73

types of, 74–75
Financial assets, 23
Financial goals. *See also* Financial advisors; Retirement planning
    asset allocation and, 45–46
    benchmarks for, 56–58
    budgeting process for achieving, 125–130
    current status, determination of, 22–24
    decision-making process for, 62
    failure, causes of, 42–43
    fear and greed impacting, 66–67
    risk assessment of, 32, 64, 65–69
    self-evaluation questions on, 19–20
    short vs. long term, 28
    specificity and measurability of, 26, 27, 30
Financial Industry Regulatory Authority (FINRA), 74
Financial planners, 74
Fixed income investments, 45
Four Percent Rule for withdrawal rates, 56–57
Functional medicine, 82

G
Gatekeepers, 137
General securities representatives, 74
Gilbert, Daniel T., 88
Goals
    action plans for, 38–43
    advisors for, 72–79. *See also* Financial advisors; Medical advisors
    applicability of, 38
    assets protection and, 23, 51–55
    benchmarks for, 56–59
    current status, determination of, 22–25
    decision-making process for, 60–63
    happiness, 86–90. *See also* Happiness
    health, 80–83. *See also* Health; Health and medical goals
    Master Trip Planner for, 91–97
    measurability of, 26–27, 28, 30, 38
    modes of change, 44–50
    process for defining, 5–7
    relevancy of, 39
    risk assessment of, 64–71
    self-evaluation questions for determining, 8–21
    short vs. long term, 28

specificity of, 26–27, 28, 30, 38
time frame for achieving, 39
visualization of, 99, 100
wealth, 84–85. *See also* Financial goals
work and career, 12–13
"Great Society" program, 31
Greed, impact on financial goals, 66–67
Guardianship papers, 111

H
Happiness, 86–90
ability to experience, 6, 89–90
barriers to, 87–88
health, relationship with, 14
methods for improving, 88–89
positive psychology on, 88
success and, 86–87
Happiness (Ben-Shahar), 89
The Happiness Advantage (Achor), 86
Happiness journals, 89
Hard assets, 46
Harvard University, 86–87, 91–92
Health, 80–83. *See also* Health and medical goals
aging, effects of, 36, 80
enhancing measures, 82–83
foundational pillars of, 29, 81–82
happiness and productivity, relationship with, 14
paths for achieving, 80, 83
Health and medical goals. *See also* Medical advisors
age management strategies, 33–36
barriers to, 61
benchmarks for, 56
current status, determination of, 22, 24
decision-making process for, 60–62
failure, causes of, 42–43
preventive plans for, 58–59
risk assessment, 64, 66, 70–71
self-evaluation questions on, 13–19, 20
specificity and measurability of, 26–27, 28, 30
Health care declarations, 107
Health care proxies, 106, 108
Health care surrogates, 106

Health insurance, 70–71
Health long term care insurance, 134
Health savings accounts (HSAs), 71
Heuristics, 60
Holdcroft, L. Thomas, 87
Holistic medicine, 78
Home equity financing, 121
Home mortgages, 121
Homeopathic physicians, 78
Hormone optimization, 81
HSAs (health savings accounts), 71

I

Imagination, power of, 99–100
Income reduction disability, 54
Income statements, 125, 127
Income tax returns, 23
Inflation, 57, 65, 124
Information-processing rules, 60
Inheritance, 23. *See also* Estate planning
Institute of Functional Medicine, 82
Insurance
    disability, 53–55, 66
    health, 70–71
    long term care, 55, 66, 133–138
    tips for reducing spending on, 121
Insurance agents, 74
Integrative wellness physicians, 78
Interest rate risk, 65
Inter vivos trusts, 109–111
Investment Advisers Act of 1940, 75
Investment portfolios, 45, 123
Investment risk, 32, 64, 65, 66–69

J

Joints, effects of aging on, 36
Journaling, 89
Jung, Carl, 6, 83

K

Killingsworth, Matthew A., 88

L

Letters of instruction, 109
Liabilities, 23, 85
"Life Between Lives" (Newton), 83
Life expectancy, 31–33
Life long term care insurance, 134
Living trusts, 109–111
Living wills, 107–108
Loan consolidation, 121
Long term care (LTC) insurance, 55, 66, 133–138
Long term goals, 28

M

Mammograms, 24
Market risk, 32
Market timing, 68–69
Master Trip Planner, 91–97
Measurability of goals, 26–27, 28, 30, 38
Medical advisors
    finding and selecting, 47–49
    types of, 77–79
    wellness teams, 47, 59, 71
Medical goals. *See* Health and medical goals
Medical insurance, 70–71
Medical power of attorney (MPOA), 106–107
Medicare, 31
Memory and cognition, effects of aging on, 36
Mental energy, 82
Modes of change, 44–50
Monetary goals. *See* Financial goals
Moody's insurance ratings, 135
Mortgages, 121
MPOA (medical power of attorney), 106–107
Muscles, effects of aging on, 36
Mutual funds, 67

N
Naturopathic physicians, 78
Near term goals, 28
Nervous system, 99, 100
Newton, Michael, 83
Non-personal assets, 52
Nurse practitioners (NPs), 77
Nursing home insurance. *See* Long term care (LTC) insurance
Nutritional health, 81–82
Nutritional supplements, 71
Nutritionists, 79

O
Osteopaths, 78
Own occupation disability, 54

P
Paralysis by analysis, 22
PAs (physician assistants), 77
Past life regression therapy, 83
Pensions, 23
Personal assets, 51–52
Physical exams, 24, 71
Physician assistants (PAs), 77
Physicians
    anti-aging/regenerative medicine specialists, 79
    family medicine, 77–78
    finding and selecting, 47–49
    holistic providers, 78
Pooled benefits, 136
Positive psychology, 88
Preventive health plans, 58–59
Probate, 110
Productivity, relationship with health, 14
Professional goals, 12–13
Prostate screening, 24
Psyche, 82

Q
Quality of life, 1, 33. *See also* Financial goals; Health and medical goals

R

Reactive health modes, 47
Recurrent claims, 137
Reduced paid-up options, 137
Regenerative medicine specialists, 79
Registered investment advisors (RIAs), 75
Registered representatives, 74
Reinvestment risk, 65–66
Relevancy of goals, 39
Residual disability, 54
Retirement planning, 120–124
    benchmarks for, 56–58
    demographic changes impacting, 31–32
    investing for growth, 123–124
    portfolio review, 123
    savings, tips for extending, 120–123
    specificity and measurability of goals, 27
Return of premium at death options, 138
Reverse mortgages, 121
Revocable trusts, 109–111
RIAs (registered investment advisors), 75
Risk assessment, 64–71
    financial, 32, 64, 65–69
    health, 64, 66, 70–71
    of market timing, 68–69

S

Salary-based financial advisors, 75
S&P 500® index, 67, 68–69
Savings
    emergency reserve, 131–132
    tips for extending, 120–123
Securities and Exchange Commission (SEC), 74, 75
Self-evaluation questions
    on financial goals, 19–20
    on goals and vision, 8–21
    on health and medical goals, 13–19, 20
    on health insurance, 70
    Master Trip Planner, 91–97
    on values, 8
    on work and career goals, 12–13
Self Regulatory Organization (SRO), 74

Seligman, Martin, 88
Short term goals, 28
Side letters, 109
SMART (specific, measurable, applicable, relevant, time) goals, 38–39
Social Security Act of 1965, 31
Social security system, 31, 32, 53
Specificity of goals, 26–27, 28, 30, 38
Spending patterns, 121–123
Springing durable power of attorney, 106
SRO (Self Regulatory Organization), 74
Standard & Poor's insurance ratings, 135
Standby durable power of attorney, 106
Stock brokers, 74
Success, relationship with happiness, 86–87
Supplements, nutritional, 71

T
Tax-qualified policies, 136
Tax returns, 23
Testamentary letters, 109
Time frame for achieving goals, 39
Time poverty, 89
Trusts, 109–111
TV consultants, 71

U
Urinary system, effects of aging on, 36

V
Values
    consistency with behaviors, 6–7, 38
    self-evaluation questions on, 8
Vision. *See* Goals
Visualization of goals, 99, 100

W
Waiting periods for benefits, 136
Waiver of premiums, 137
Wealth, 84–85. *See also* Financial goals
Weiss, Brian, 83

Wellness teams, 47, 59, 71. *See also* Medical advisors
Wills, 108–109
Withdrawal rates, 56–57, 66
Work and career goals, 12–13
Worry, as barrier to happiness, 87

CPSIA information can be obtained at www.ICGtesting.com
Printed in the USA
BVOW04s1235010614

354971BV00001B/2/P

9 781478 723561